"This Project has been co-sponsored by a grant from the Middlesex County Cultural and Heritage Commission/ Board of Chosen Freeholders, through funding in part from the New Jersey State Council on the Arts/Department of State, a Partner Agency of National Endowment for the Arts, and the Wallace Foundation."

INDO-AMERICAN LITERARY ACADEMY, USA

ANTHOLOGY OF POEMS (2005)

IN

ENGLISH, HINDI, GUJARATI & MARATHI

:: EDITOR -IN-CHIEF ::
Prof. Chandrakant P. Desai
Founder & Convener,
Indo-American Literary Academy, USA
1, Lindsey Ct., Franklin Park, NJ 08823, USA
Phone : (732) 821 - 1272

INDO-AMERICAN LITERARY ACADEMY'S
ANTHOLOGY OF POEMS (2005)

*

© *Indo-American Literary Academy*

*

First Edition : 2005

*

Price : $12.00

*

:: *Publisher* ::
INDO-AMERICAN LITERARY ACADEMY
1, Lindsey CT. Franklin Park, NJ 08823, U.S.A.
(732) 821 - 1272

*

:: *Book Distributer (India)* ::
SUMAN BOOK CENTRE
88, Princess Street, Anand Bhavan Building,
Mumbai - 400 002. Tel. : 2205 6305
E-mail : sumanbc@rediffmail.com

*

I.S.B.N.No. 0-9634271-4-8

*

: *Type Setting* :
TANISHQ CREATIONS
Dombivli, Thane - 421 202 (India)

*

: *Printer* :
KONAM PRINTERS
Tardeo, Mumbai - 400 034. (India)

INDO-AMERICAN LITERARY ACADEMY, USA

ANTHOLOGY OF POEMS (2005)
IN
English, Hindi, Gujarati & Marathi

* <u>Editor-in-Chief : Prof. Chandrakant P. Desai</u> *

* <u>Editorial Committee (English Poems)</u> *

Prof. Chandrakant P. Desai * Monika Y. Chokshi

* <u>Editorial Committee (Hindi Poems)</u> *

Dr. Govardhan Sharma * Dr. Anjana Sandhir
Dr. Hemant Sharma

* <u>Editorial Committee (Gujarati Poems)</u> *

Prof. Chandrakant P. Desai * Pravin Patel (Shashi)
Sarla Vyas * Subodh Shah

* <u>Editorial Committee (Marathi Poems)</u> *

Dilip Chitre * Ashok Vidwans

* Publisher & Distributor (USA) *
Indo-American Literary Academy
1 Lindsey Court, Franklin Park, NJ 08823-1525, USA
Phone : (732) 821-1272

3

STATE OF NEW JERSEY
OFFICE OF THE GOVERNOR
P.O. BOX 001
TRENTON
08625
(609) 292-6000

RICHARD J. CODEY
ACTING GOVERNOR

July 1, 2005

Dear Friends,

It is my pleasure to extend warm greetings and offer my congratulations to the members of the Indo-American Literary Academy on the publishing of *The Anthology of Poems (2005).*

The arts enrich the lives of all Americans, affecting every aspect of life in America today. New Jersey strives to develop and support artistic talent, while presenting opportunities for individuals to perform and showcase their many talents. The arts significantly enhance the quality of life culturally, socially, and aesthetically for all our residents.

On behalf of the Sate of New Jersey, I would like to recognize the efforts and talents of the members of the Indo-American Literary Academy, and commend their commitment to furthering the arts within the Garden State. The residents of New Jersey are truly fortunate to benefit from such individuals.

Once again, congratulations and best hopes for the future. My Administration is committed to providing a State government that works for all the people of New Jersey. With stability and dignity, we have the power to make our lives better.

With regards,

Richard J. Codey
Acting Governor

4 : ANTHOLOGY OF POEMS (2005)

This Indo-American Literary Academy's Anthology of Poems (2005) is dedicated to

* The greatest NRI Mahatma Gandhi, who lived two & a half decades out of India and returned to win freedom for India, practising & preaching truth & non-violence to the people of India & the World.

* Mohini Mohun Chatterji, distinguished author of the book "BHAGAVAD GITA or THE LORD'S LAY" (published by Houghton Mifflin Co. in 1887), translated from Sanskrit into English with commentary, notes and references to the Christian scriptures; thereby introducing Indian cultural heritage to the people of USA.

* Swami Vivekananda, who addressed The All Religions Conference in Chicago, Illinois in 1893 creating interest and respect for the Indian culture.

* Prof. Albert Einstein, great admirer of Mahatma Gandhi and his vision of Truth and Non-violence in the service of mankind.

* Dr. Martin Luther King Jr. who took inspiration from Mahatma Gandhi's life and doctrine of truth, non-violence and practice of civil disobedience in

his struggle against evil and social injustice.

* Honorable President John F. Kennedy, a great friend of India and admirer of Indian culture.

* Dr. Bharat S. Shah, Dr. Anjana Sandhir, Mrs. Panna Naik, Mrs. Rajni Bhargava and others either involved in writing Text-Books for the Indo-American Younger generation, to learn Gujarati, Hindi & other Indian languages; and/or involved in teaching Indian languages.

* Mr. Ramanbhai Patel, who was the first Indo-American most probably in the early 20th century, to enter into the ownership and operation of the motels/hotels, thereby becoming the pioneer in the hospitality industry for the Indo-Americans, who inherited hospitality from the Indian culture. Now almost 40% to 50% of the motels/hotels in the USA, are owned and operated by the Indo-Americans, who promote the Indian vision of hospitality in the USA.

* Mr. Sam Pitroda with whose dedicated service, in the field of Telecommunication to our Motherland India, almost every home has a telephone and every person has a mobile phone, boosting the national economy and lifting up the life of the people.

* All the poets, who contributed their poems for the Anthology.

Inspite of we Indians migrated to USA, having English as its national language, we still write literature in our Indian languages and some of us write in English too. In The United States, there are various literary organizations and groups dealing in various Indian languages. They have their activities mostly limited to the same language speaking people. Although such activities please and satisfy our sentiments for our mothertongue, culture and people, at the same time we feel that we are missing something very vital. Afterall we are living not only in a village or town, state or nation; but also in a continent and on the planet Earth, which is just a small fraction of the universe. Keeping this in view, The Indo-American Literary Academy promotes interfacing of the poets & writers writing in different Indian languages and English, as well as promotes the interaction of the literature in different Indian languages and English, the latter one being the International language, in addition to being the national language of USA. This Anthology of Poems (2005) in four languages, namely English, Hindi, Gujarati and Marathi; is an humble step in that direction.

Through this Anthology, the poets and writers will get an opportunity to become familiar with the poets &

poetry of languages other than their own; and to communicate with them directly on one to one basis. This will broaden our thoughts and understanding, and this Kind of phenomenon will be benificial to the literature in general. This has a positive impact on the peace of the region as well as the world. We can not ignore the fact that we are living in the era of spacetravel, wherein the mankind is communicating with the moon and mars other planets and stars, may be millions of light years away from our globe of Earth.

When I meet the poets, writers & organizers of different literary groups of Indian languages in USA, I see a kind of anxiety on their faces, telling me "Will the Indian languages survive in USA?" Let us examine this question, in order to derive an answer. First of all, when we observe the Indian language literary meetings, we notice that they look like Senior Citizens Association meetings, younger generation almost absent. We live with them, but we are unable to inspire them to attend the meetings. In general, we lack communication with our next & us-born generation. we should take more interest in their problems of life & language; and they will reciprocate with double spirit. We should take interest in them quite positively and not just superfluously. If they happily take Spanish or French at the schools, why not Indian languages? I have seen our US-born Youngsters taking Hindi or Gujarati at their schools and they should have no problem in attending the literary meetings, in which their parents or grandparents take interest and participate. Such two or three generations participation in the Indian literary events will increase the chances of survival of the Indian languages and their literature.

Right now only four languages have been considered in this Anthology of poems(2005). But the Academy has a future plan to accommodate other Indian languages too, marching toward the ideal of सर्वभाषा सरस्वती (Goddess of knowledge dwells in all languages). Ofcourse it is quite a novel approach and a challenge. But with the cooperation of the Indo-American poets & writers of different Indian languages, it is possible to meet the challenge.

The Academy's Objectives and the brief overview of the Academy's literary meetings held at The Barnes & Noble Bookstore, North Brunswick, NJ will better explain how the Academy has steadily progressed toward its goal, and benifited the Indo-American people in their literary pursuit. The Academy appeals the Indo-American poets, writers and literary talents to form broadbased literary groups of common interest and operate their activities at the nearest Barnes & Noble Bookstore, feeling free to name their literary group, if they wish, as Indo-American Literary Academy of the city or state in which they meet; thus forming hundreds of such Academies promoting Indo-American Literary interest in various Indian languages plus English; thereby also promoting Indian cultural heritage through literary accomplishment.

The Academy heartily thanks The Middlesex County Cultural & Heritage Commission and The Board of Chosen Freeholders for providing the grant for the production of this Anthology of Poems (2005). Also thanks are due to Ms. Isha Vyas & Ms. Bethany Wildrich for their help and suggestions for this Anthology - project. At this juncture, it's very appropriate to extend special thanks from the Academy to the community relations managers Dr. Debbie Cutchin, Ms. Ann Eisenhut and other managerial staff of the Barnes & Noble Bookstore, North Brunswick of Middlesex County, NJ for their valuable cooperation in arranging Academy's meetings, since June 2001.

The Academy is pleased to extend its sincere thanks to all the members of the editorial committees for their valuable contribution in bringing up the quality of the Anthology, at the same time reflecting the Indo-American vision and diversity of the topics. Special thanks are also due to Ms. Preety Sengupta, Prof. Shanti

Tangri, Mr. Ramesh Tambe, Mrs. Manisha Chokshi, Mr. Yogesh Chokshi, Mrs. Swati Gandhi and Mrs. Nila Desai for their useful suggestions and cooperation in bringing up this Anthology. Last but not the least, the Academy thanks to all the participating poets without whose contribution of quality poems, this Anthology-project would not have been successful.

Lastly the Academy thanks all those, who actively supported the Academy; some of the names to mention are: Pravin Patel (Shashi), Subodh Shah, Dr. Hemant Sharma, Nila Desai, Sarla & Avinash Vyas, Bhagesh Kadakia, Shankar Patel, Ashok Vidwans, Hon. Assemblyman Mr. Upendra Chivukula, Hon. Ex-Mayor of Franklin Twp. Ms. Shirley Eberly, Ms. Edith Kaltovich president and Tony Hwilka Vice-President of New Jersey Poetry Society, Hasmukh Barot & Ramesh Jadav of Gujarat Times, Suman Mozumdar of India Abroad, Subhash Shah of Gujarat Darpan, Nitin Gurjar of Tiranga in NJ, Kishore Desai of Gurjari, G.M. Shroff, Jalendu Vaidya, J.V. Sheth, Shobhan Bantwal, Prof. Jagadish Vyas, Prof. Bipin Sangankar, Shirish Shastri, Himanshu Pathak, Sudhakar Bhatt, Shashikant Desai and all those whom I may have missed to mention.

Prof. Chandrakant P. Desai
Founder & Convener of The
Indo-American Literary Academy.

BRIEF OUTLINE OF THE LITERARY ACTIVITIES OF THE INDO-AMERICAN LITERARY ACADEMY AT BARNES & NOBEL BOOKSTORE, NORTH BRUNSWICK, (MIDDLESEX COUNTRY) NEW JERSEY.

1. Inauguration of Chandrakant Desai's book of poems "Amari Ameri Galiman" and discussion on it; open poetry reading in any Indian language or English (6-19-2001).

2. Presentation of book "Helen Keller's Life" by Bhagesh Kadakia and discussion by the author; Presentation of the book of poems "Tankho" by Dr. Rasik Pandya and discussion by the author, followed by open poetry & prose reading (7-17-2001).

3. Presentation & discussion on the book "Ek Pankhi Na Pinchhu Saat" (Travels in Central America) by Preety Sengupta, followed by open Poetry and prose Reading in any Indian language or English (8-21-2001).

4. Presentation & discussion on the books "Savitri Ek Adhyayan" and "Savitri No Yog" by the author Prof. Jagadish Vyas (Epic Savitri was written by Maharshi Aurobindo Ghosh), followed by peotry/prose reading by the attending poets & writers (9-18-2001).

5. Presentation & discussion on the book "Kavyadhara" collection of poems by the author Mr. Pravin Patel (Shashi), followed by open poetry / prose reading by attending poets & writers (10-16-2001).

6. Poets & writers read their poems/prose related to Sept. 11 tragedy, human rights, world peace etc. (11-20-2001).

7. In honor of Martin Luther King's Birthday, the poets & writers discuss similarities between his and Gandhi's philosophies of non-violence and civil disobedience (1-6-2002).

8. Celebration of Black History month and Freedom Day; Discussion by the audience on "Respect for the people of all religions and Democracy (2-3-2002).

9. Celebration of National women's History Month; discussion by the attending poets and writers on "Uplifting of women and all oppressed people of the world. (03-03-2002)

10. Observing the National child Abuse Prevention Month and National. D.A.R.E Day; there was a discussion on human rights and improving social life of children of the world(4-7-2002).

11. Celebration of the International Year of Mountains (2002) as declared by the United Nations; open poetry reading by attending poets on the mountain related topics (5-5-2002).

12. Presentation & discussion on the Pulitzer prize winning book "Interpreter of Maladies" by Jhumpa Lahiri; the discussion was led by speakers from NAMI & SAMHAJ (6-2-2002).

13. Presentation & discussion by the author Ms. Nirmala Moorthy of her Novel "The Coiled Serpent" followed by Open Poetry Reading by the attending Poets (7-7-2002).

14. Prof. Bipin Sangankar led the discussion on "The International influence of Lord Mahavir's Message of Non-violence on people and Literature of the World". This program was organized to comemorate Lord Mahavir's 2600th Birthday(8-4-2002).

15. Prof. Chandrakant P. Desai led the literary discourse & discussion on "The direction in which Indo-American poetry is going, with a special reference to poetry in the Gujarati language", followed by Open Poetry Reading in any indian language or English(9-1-2002).

16. Paying tribute to the victims of Sept.11; Honoring Mr. Tarun Patel Indo-American, who joined the US Army and served in Afghanistan. Franklin Twp. Mayor Ms. Eberly and Assembleyman Mr. Chivukula were the Hon. Guests. Open Poetry Reading then followed (10-6-2002).

17. Prof. Chandrakant P.Desai gave a talk & discussion on "The Art of writing Gazals" as interpreted by eminent poets "Shunya Palanpuri, Hemant Desai & Chinu Modi" followed by Open Poetry Reading (11-3-2002).

18. Presentation and discussion of the Novel "The Seduction of Silence" by the author Ms.Bem Le Hunte, followed

by open peotry/prose Reading in any Indian language or English(2-2-2003).

19. Presentation and discussion on his Novel "Vanshveli"as well as on the different dimensions of fiction in Hindi by the eminent Hindi writer Dr. Govardhan Sharma, followed by Open Poetry Reading (8-17-2003).

20. Prof. Chandrakant P. Desai led the discussion on the latest Novel "The Namesake" by the pulitzer Prizewinning author Ms. Jhumpa Lahiri, followed by Open Peotry Reading(3-26-2004).

21. Celebration of National poetry Month.Eminent writer of Humor in India, Prof. Bakul Tripathi introduced his book "Humor : Friendship with God" and presented some of his humorous poems and humor pieces. Ms.Edith Kaltovich introduced New Jersey poetry Society's Anthology of poems "Seeds for April's Sowing". Open Poetry Reading followed the above program (4-23-2004).

22. National Poetry Day Celebration. Prof. Niranjan Bhagat, top-ranking poet and writer from India gave a presentation titled "Indian peotry: Its place in the World literature and its relationship with American Poetry" and read some of his poems in Gujarati and English. Ms. Edith Kaltovich president of The New Jersey Poetry Society read some of her poems and introduced Society's activities. The Open Poetry Reading followed the above program (9-12-2004).

23. *Paying tribute to the victims of Tsunami Disaster; Readings of Prayers from all the Religions; Announcement of the publication of The Academy's Anthology of Poems (2005) in English, Hindi, Gujarati and Marathi, in cooperation with The Middlesex County Cultural and Heritage Commission; and Open Poetry Reading (2-6-2005).*

24. *Mrs. Suparna Guha, director and Coordinator of The Indian Institite of Performing Arts gave a presentation on "Rabindranath Tagore : On Retrospects" and sang some of Tagore's poems with Rabindra Sangit, as part of the celebration of Indo-American Poetry Month(May is Tagore's Birth-month). Mrs. Sabari Ghosh delivered Rabindra Sangit. Eminent Poet & writer Mrs. Preety Sengupta inaugurated the English Novel "The Ordeal of Innocence" by Popular Indian writer Mr. Jayanti M. Dalal; Mr. Dalal spoke about his Novel. Eminent Hindi writer Dr. Govardhan Sharma inaugurated Mrs. Preety Sengupta's book "Our India" containing over 480 pictures of sites, buildings, temples, religious and historical places etc. presenting the Indian Culture, followed by a talk by the author Mrs. Sengupta. Open Poetry Reading followed the above program(5-8-2005).*

Note : All Open Poetry Readings mentioned above were open for poetry/prose readings in any indian language or English.

SONG OF THE UNITED STATES OF AMERICA

We are the humble humans
Proud Patriots
Great Americans
And worthy world citizens.

Our soil is sacred
And waters are mineral honey,
Our air is filled with princely perfumes,
And clouds have golden & silver linings,
Our wealthy forest are colored heaven in spring and fall,
Great Rocky & Appalachian Mountains are
The lovely breasts of our motherland
Feeding our lives since ages.

Thundering Atlantic & peaceful Pacific throb in our hearts
And our great rivers
Mississippi & Missouri, Ohio & Colorado,
Arkansas, Tennessee, Hudson & Potomac
Flow in our blood steadily & vigorously.

Cool breezes from the parks & lakes
Envelop our lives
Like the pulp over the nuts.

We are the sporty Yankees & Knicks,
Bulls & Bears, Ravens & Lakers,

Cowboys & Devils, 49ers & 76ers,
And many more Giants.
We may loose or win,
But our spirit is always up & never down.

We love & care for
Our kids boundless
Our elders endless
And our families with affection no less.

Our beautiful America glitters
With the shining rainbow colors:
White, black, yellow, brown, red & several others.
Beauty of the rainbow is not just in heaven,
Its on the earth too.
Behind all these colors
Is the one single crystal clear color
Of the rays of the supreme sun our gracious God
Who dwells in all the lives,
All the races and religions.
And blesses with enormous grace
Not just our nation, but the entire world.

Heartstrings of our homeland are interwoven with
Hometowns & ranches of red Indians,
Washington Roads & Lincoln Highways,
Kennedy Boulevards & Jackson Streets,
Joyce Kilmer Road & Walt Whitman center,

Robert Frost's lovely, dark & deep woods,
Einstein Avenue & Edison Tower,
M.L.King Boulevards & Mahatma Gandhi Plaza,
Franklin & Roosevelt Parks,
Several Six flags & Disneys spilling with thousand funs,
Beautiful beaches adorned with wonderful waves,
And many more countless silken fibers.

Since centuries
A lady descended from heaven
Sings the songs of liberty & love.
She holds a sparkling torch in her hand
And world embracing light in her eyes.
In the tumultuous waters of Hudson,
She stands tall & gorgeous, gazing at
The thundering & jumping waves of the Atlantic.

Her heart is longing for the children
From all over the world,
Who are crushed & crumbled
Having hidden hopes in their hearts.
She wipes their tears
And embraces them with sky like love
And welcomes them
On the land of the free & home of the brave
In the soothing & beautiful America.
For many decades
This lady of Liberty standing in the Hudson waters

Affectionately watched the tall twin towers.
Although they disappeared behind the evil shadow
Both are still studded in her eager eyes.
With the magic of her vigorous vision
They will soon awake shaking off the dust & the ashes
And will multiply & appear again
Taller & grander
Trading & tripling the American wealth,
And that of the world too.
Make no mistake
We toss the terrors with our toes
And cross any mountains blocking our Path.

Again & again let us loudly proclaim
With the thundering roar filling the sky
That we are the humble humans, proud patriots, great
Americans
And worthy world citizens
Blessed by the God Almighty in whom we trust.

- Chandrakant P. Desai

Note : Prof. Chandrakant Desai is the first Indo-American poet invited to read his patriotic poem at the inaugaral function at Capitol Hill, Washington D.C., a day before newly elected congress started working in January 2003.

INDO-AMERICAN LITERARY ACADEMY

Convener : Prof. Chandrakant P. Desai

1 Lindsey Court, Franklin Park NJ 08823, USA

Phone: (732) 821 1272

Date: 7th June 2001

:: OBJECTIVES ::

(1) For its literary activities, presently the Academy meets at *BARNES & NOBEL* Book Store located at 869 Route 1 South, North Brunswick, NJ 08902., Phone: (732)545-7966. The nature and detail of the literary meetings will be announced in the *BARNES & NOBEL'S* Monthly Events Listing; as well as fliers mailed to those interested in the Academy's activities.

(2) To Promote and encourage Indo-American people to write or take interest in the poetry, fiction, non-fiction etc. in the languages of India & English on the topics & themes concerning Indo-American Life.

(3) To promote translation of literary works of eminent Indian poets & writers, from Indian languages into English; in order to give glimpses of Indian literary wealth reflecting Indian life and culture to the Indo-American and American people, as well as the world at large. It is worth noting that, if *GITANJALI* had not been translated into English, the world would not have known the beauty & wealth of the literature of Ravindranath Tagore, and that he would not have won the nobel prize.

(4) Indians in America can not and should not isolate themselves from the American main stream, and

try to contribute substantially to the Indo-American literature, in order to develop mutual understanding among the people of diverse origin, as well to enrich America with the precious Indian cultural heritage.

(5) To bring forth or to bring in lime light the literary works of Indo-American poets & writers, so that their writings may rich out to the American & Indo-American community scattered almost all over the 50 states of USA.

(6) Mahatma Gandhi's philsophy of life interwoven with truth & non-violence, peace & love has been now widely accepted by the world including USA. This academy shall encourage Indo-American & other American poets and writers to promote Gandhian literature befitting the needs of the 21st century.

(7) Almost all the Indian languages including Hindi, Gujarati, Punjabi, Marathi, Bengoli, Tamil etc. are spoken and written by the Indoamerican people. It is interesting to note that Spanish, Chinese and Japanese have received considerable attention und got considerable US recognition. This Academy shall work for the similar US recognition of one or more Indian languages.

(8) To promote poetry reading, Kavi-sammelan/Mushayara, drama and literary discussions in various Indian languages, with special attention to Indoamerican interest. The Academy will also promote and encourage movie making reflecting Indo-American interest.

(9) To promote writing of the Text-books teaching Indian languages to the US born and raised Indo-American generation and interested Americans, in order to bring them in touch with the unparallel beauty, values and

vast literature treasured in those languages.

(10) To encourage US born & raised generation and others to read poetry, fiction and nonfiction in original Indian languages, as well as to write & communicate in indian languages, where and when needed. while promoting the indain languages, we can not ignore the fact that English is widely spoken & written all over India and ofcourse in USA, which is the melting pot of different cultures of the world.

(11) In order to promote the literary activities in different indian languages, on need basis, the academy will nominate one convener for each language, who will work for and orginaze literary activities of Indo-American interest in that language.

(12) In order to promote the literary activities in different areas of USA, if needed, the Academy may establish different area Academies of USA; each area convener will conduct and organize literary activities of Indoamerican interest in that area.

(13) Depending on the future growth of literary acivities, the Academy will develop necessary organizational structure, to systematize and organize Academy's activities, in order to meet the demand of the future growth. The Academy is a non-profit group.

(14) To support literary activities in Indian languages, performed by other organizations or persons. Suggestions are welcome from friends and others having IndoAmerican interest.

Chandrakant P. Desai
Founder & convener,
IndoAmerican Literary Academy, USA

CONTENT

ENGLISH POEMS

26 : ANTHOLOGY OF POEMS (2005)

HINDI POEMS

GUJARATI POEMS

30 : ANTHOLOGY OF POEMS (2005)

INDO-AMERICAN LITERARY ACADEMY'S

ANTHOLOGY OF POEMS (2005)

ENGLISH SECTION

GLORY

The music from the Stars,
The songs I hear from the horizons,
You've composed the tunes of your presence,
The evening celebrates the streams of memories.
The universe moves on to the expanding sky,
This is the play of God —the Supreme Being.

In the play, He remains unseen and unknowable,
His presence I feel in this celebration,
The evenig points where He is,
Just finding Him is my innovation.
Let's move on towards the destination,
The celebration isn't over yet,
I ought to find the light of His glory.

-Bharat Thakkar

THE BIRD

In the dark midnight,
Why did the peace fly away
Like a bird in the wildness?
It disturbed the nests.
The budding flowers stopped blooming,
The mystical peace left
The region of my mind.

Where do I find that bird?
In the churches, mosques or temples,
In my heart,
From the river to ocean,
In the sky,
From horizons to my home,
It flew away far,
Very far beyond the infinity.

How would I even know
If I find that bird?
Its wings are fresh, morning's delight,
Its colors are brighter that the sun,
Its soaring silence deepens in my mind,
When it comes,
The divine overflows in the heart.

- *Bharat Thakkar*

Bhumika Desai

C/o Jalendu Vaidya, 105 Fornelius Ave. Clifton, NJ 07013; she loves writing poems in English; she is a second year college student at Rutgers state University, NJ.

A PRESENT FOR YOU

If I don't say your name tonight
If I don't think of you today
If I forget your existence
Will you still be there when I awake ?
If I prolong my time on other things
If I fall asleep
If I leave the country
If I go fishing
If I discover the nature of brahman
If I am conscious of only consciousness
If I built a time machine and erased the day
You were
If I made a hole my hide-away
If I left a sign saying "closed"
Would you still be determining my fate ?
All I'm asking is a little refrain
A small favor in the least
Would you deny me such a wish
All I ask is for a break
From thought
From action
From mind
As my eyes become heavy I look at you
You beckon…smiling
I hate you
Two more hours
Then sleep awaits
Till tomorrow the rest will wait

- Bhumika Desai

Bulusu Lakshman

1406, Mindy Lane, Piscataway, NH 08854. In his early school-years, he was enthralled by the work of great poets. This inspired him to write poems. His poems have appeared in various magazines, journals and anthologies in The United States & India. His one collection of poems has been published. He is listed as a poet in the Directory of American Poets & Fiction Writers. He is a software professional.

FOREVER BEAUTIFUL

Life anew is beautiful
Small wonders are beautiful
Love and lovely smiles few
A moment of happiness too.

Live in love, live life to the full,
The many memories are but unforgetful
Life's little secrets are priceless presents
Accept them and create timeless moments

Nature is beauty's form made real
To the eye of the beholder a sight indeed ideal
A unique blend of perfection and art it does conceal
To one and all, heart-in-heart it does appeal

Near and dear are seemingly close
Accept them to see how affection grows
Hand-in-hand with them gives a real pleasure
Their love for sure is a veritable treasure

Everything good transcends goodness
Enriches life to the extent of Godliness
All of this is beautiful, very beautiful
Not just beautiful, FOREVER BEAUTIFUL

— *Bulusu Lakshman*

GOOD, BETTER, BEST

Whatever is good, better, best
Stands above all of the rest

A child, to the mother, is always the best
Lying in her folded arms, cuddled on her chest

So is the fledgling to the bird in the nest
Warm and protective, like an inner worn vest

Love remains superlative is what these suggest
Love and loved ones are more than the best

Leave place for compromise and request
Whether dealing with self, someone or guest

Get possessed with zeal or zest
Get obsessed to reach the crest

When life gets tough, comes the real test
Put yourself to test and conquer the quest

The only way to get the best
Is to arise, awake and do one's best

Good is always gateway to the best
Good turns to better and ends in best

- *Bulusu Lakshman*

OUR HEARTBEATS

Our heartbeats are interwoven
With the finest fibres of two great Homelands,
One is India, the ancient home of great culture
And another The United States of America,
The new land of modern western culutre.

India is the mother of great ancient civilization,
Enriched with high cultural and spiritual values,
Birthplace of four great religions,
Next door neighbour of the great Himalaya Mountains
And several wonders of the world including
Tajmahal of beautiful marble stones
And Mahatma Gandhi, Apostle of truth and non-violence.

United States of America,
The great land of the free and home of the brave,
The treasure of innumerable opportunities and wealth,
Enriched with the great values of liberty and equality,
Following the footsteps of the great Abe Lincoln
With the Government of the people, for the people,
By the people.

Marvelous Mumbai and Manhattan,
Both are studded in our eyes,
We love Newyorker pizza,
But can't forget the great taste of Chowpati's Bhelpuri;
Our dollar balance jumps high,
But the Rupees are still rolling in our mind.

We enjoy Trick and Treat,
Helloween candies and costumes;

However our heart still gets sprayed
By the beautiful colors and songs of Holi featival.

Often we swim in the dancing waves of Atlantic and Pacific;
But in our dreams,
We swim in the welcoming waves of the Indian ocean,
And in the sacred waters of Ganga, Yamuna,
And many more.

We see the sacred Narmada, Tapi, Godavari, Kaveri,
In the tumultuous waters of Hudson, Tennessee, Mississippi.
Our life blended with the great values of the East and West,
Finds Stars in the Tricolor
And Gandhi in Lincoln and King.

Our vision is expanding beyond the four walls of our home,
And we long for a greater home
With sky as its ceiling and earth as its living room,
Shining with the Chandeliers of the sun, moon and mars,
Where we can host the entire universe
Without any exception.

- Chandrakant P. Desai

AUTOBIOGRAPHY OF THE WHITEHOUSE

You missed a lot
If you haven't seen me.
Mr. President misses a lot
If he quits me abruptly;
And gets to the bottom
If he loses me by impeachment.

I emerged from freedom,
But I lamented for my incomplete whiteness;
For many years,
Until the slaves saw the light of freedom
And women got the voting right.
I am proud of my whiteness,
But it's upto Mr. President, the people
And the Government for, by and of the people
To keep me as white as snow
Without scornful scratches and filth.

Although I am a house of stones, bricks and marbles,
I am a great home of the great nation,
With a spongy heart worrying for all
Including hungry and homeless.
My eyes flood with tears,
Seeing miseries of the millions.
I cried
When the states divided
And smiled
When united.
I am ashamed,
Seeing the people discriminating themselves.
I feel happy and proud,
Seeing them loving each other.

I was amazed with boundless joy
To find Abe Lincoln dwelling in me.
He saw just one human color in all,
Unity in diversity,
I felt proud of my distinguished [P] resident,
For his farsighted vision of unconditional freedom.

I was overjoyed
When President Andrew Jackson dwelled in me,
And felt proud to learn
That he refused to polish the britishers' boots
And welcomed the wounds from them,
While he was a young POW.

I was almost shattered,
And my eyes flooded with tears,
When president Truman ordered
To shower Atom bombs on Nagasaki and Hiroshima.
What a great sin by a great human
Residing in a great house of great country ?

I am friendly with the entire world,
Even with the moon and mars and the world beyond.
I am made of solid stone, But I melted like wax,
When my [P] residents waged wars forgetting peace,
Killing thousands on either side.
The bloody wars
Though fought thousands of miles away,
Reddened my gloomy face.
I wept in wars, smiled in truce
And always craved for the peace of mankind.

I have some dark spots within me,
Although I am white from outside.
Troubled and tired, I sleep off and on, of course restless.
White washing these spots,
Some [P] residents tried their best to awaken me.
But my eyes are still drowsy,

As most of the time
They are too busy to eradicate them entirely.

May be politics or sex
Scandals are never new to me.
Whether impeached or not
Or just missing impeachment,
It certainly faded my whiteness
And dimmed my brightness to some extent.

I have seen the actor becoming the president
And some presidents behaving as actors.
Sometimes I wondered :
Am I really the white house?
Or Broadway or Hollywood ?

Civil rights bill brought me closer to people's heart
And spaceships brought me closer to moon and mars;
Its only one hour flight to united Nations,
But I am still swinging between war and peace.

So far I could host only first ladies
And I am dreaming to host woman president.
Just being white,
Doesn't mean I favor white,
I am dreaming to host colored president too.

The world knows me as white house,
But I bear variety of colors in and out .
It's a mystery to me :
Who colored it that way ?
And how it happened ?
If at all it will be known,
It could be only partly and never fully.

-Chandrakant P. Desai

HEAVEN'S GATE

I am still in my dormant state
Yet I am passing through Heaven's Gate
That's the blessing I love to hate

I slowly glide to the other side
Chasing a point of light in the night
On the wings of a long flight

I beat the fog for clear illumination
Getting so close to the center of creation
My senses are numbed with fascination

An image unfolds above the mounts
I hear the light and see the sounds
A twinkle of joy in my soul abounds

Brittled lens is in between
Can't make out the images seen
Is this the way it has always been?

The distance grows in close range
Light is the same but frames change
That's how images re-arrange

Christ or Krishna or Buddha pervades
It's the same face in changing shades
It alone dwells when all else fades

I must seek and not be lost
Criss of the images are all crossed
Call it dew or call it frost

Lonesome again in the same hemisphere
Time to return is drawing near
A shadow till then but now the seer

To catch that speck I can't wait
All things from that point radiate
The light is on this side of Heaven's Gate

- *Dhananjaya Kumar*

FLASH

Are we all made up of the same matter?
Our cells communicate with one another
Left hand moves when the right one pains
Is someone happy when anyone gains?

Soft bread we chew, hard one they swallow
Is that the difference when no meals to follow?
Land is uneven or rain clouds wander
Here comes the master of nature to surrender

That was the mother, this is the daughter
Both are watching in despair
One for having given, one for begotten
Of peddle and chain, one is forgotten

Losing the beats and missing the blinks
With lullaby screams and bloody dreams
Election and software are all ours
Rwands and Bosina are all theirs

Stop the rivers and bury the flowers
Fly with the winds, rip the bird's feathers
Spit in the cloud and poison the water
To live upstream is not to bother

Destiny and road-map are all in the books
The goal is near, yet the path is long
With our own sun and many other stars
The flash in our eyes shadows the light

Let's stop the time to ponder the endeavor
At least pretend that we live forever
Sow the seeds again deeper in the earth
Or show me a place of tandem worth

Our flag on the moon and needle in the heart
In quest for heaven, where do we start?
So much to overlook and so much to see
Are we all one, are we all free?

Dhananjaya Kumar

Dhara Vaidya

105 Fornelius Ave. Clifton, NJ 07013; she loves writing poems in English; she is second year college student at Montclair state University, NJ.

IN THE MIDST

Loneliness,
the sense of freedom,
the touch of hope upon a desire to walk among
the midst of the moonshine.
Laughter,
the swing of joy, the love of one to love another for
the love of oneself.
Usage of life through poverty of melody and
the thirst of poison to die in the hopes of
loneliness and a gift of love.
Towards these composite mixtures of luscious
grimes
one desires to awake in the midst of a shallow
mist of trust towards a stranger the heart has
grown loyalty for.
Those whom one runs after
but never reach,
simply to want another.
What fun!
of life
to die in the arms of yet another stranger
one's self.

- *Dhara Vaidya*

I YEARN

Dreams aside
For Just a sight
Simple radiance
Waiting at the door

Hopes unite
For just a night
Prickling a way
In the dust of a cry.

Anxious is the fear
Of joy to secrete
Pride of trust
For a stranger in time

Just a moment awaits
Then a smile of lust
Strides a lane
Belying a right

Childish may one say
Comes a thought to mind
I yearn,
See this stranger-
Again in Life ?

- Dhara Vaidya

Edith R. Kaltovich

12 Rydal Dr., Lawrencwville, NJ 08648; president of New Jersey poetry Society to which Indo-American Literary Academy is affiliated; deeply interested in Indian Poetry ; published poetry-Collections in English and Spanish; translated poetry books from Spanish to English and English to Spanish; listed in various Who-is-who Books; born in Cordoba, Argentina; retired from The Trenton Public School System; Spanish Professor adjunct At the College of New Jersey and Mercer County Community College; Past President of Arts Council, Lawrenceville, NJ ; member of various Literary organizations at Federal and state Levels.

A TRIBUTE TO INDIA

The Fifteenth of August 1947

It is the end of an old era.
It is the beginning of a new age.
India arises to achieve expansion
Greatness, Power, prosperity.
Freedom, liberation of Asia.
These aims and ideals play
In the progress of human civilization
The rise of a new, a greater,
Brighter, nobler life for mankind.
India's spiritual knowledge of life
Is a new step in the evolution
Of the many problems of existence.
India is free from the chaos
Of separate states preceded by the British conquest.
A progressive understanding of the need of peace

Moves through struggles towards freedom.
India plays her part, it begins to play it
With energy, ability to indicate the measure
Of her possiblilities, the place she can take
In the council of the nations,
India's liberation depended upon
This new and free India on that
August Fifteenth in 1947.

- *Edith R. Kaltovich*

SUN

Why sun
do you look at
me ? Do you want to dry
my tears ? Don't you see the flood in
my soul ?

A ROSE

A Rose
opens again
my dreams to all turning
limits of the thirty-two points
compass

A TRY

Try catch
the butterflies
follow, swaying, floating
my eyes see transparent colors
alone.

- Edith R. Kaltovich

NONCHALANCE

If you leave, I will fill this house
with emptiness.
I will take this opportunity to
know myself.
I blossomed with you,
Now I experience autumn.
On the waves of silence
I am drifting nonchalant.
I enjoyed your company,
Now I am disjointed in dissolution.
We'll play another round...
This fall...

- Indra shah

A NIGHT AT MAHABALESHVARA

Nature
In silent solitude
Tranquil and dreaming

The pathway shrouded
Beneath darkness
Asleep.

My heart's echoes
Fall on sleeping
Nests, birds.

E'en my footsteps
Cannot be the sleeping
Pathway-shrouded
In gloom-awake.

My songs vainly
Fall on deaf leaves-
And poorer am I,
My songs are lost to me,

The wind
As a cruel, cold, sharp
Knife
Cuts through my life.
I bleed.

A bat shrieks past
Piercing the gloom
The silence and me.
The mountains

Raise their
Obscure mighty
Heads,
Barren bossoms
And crush
My burden'd soul.

In the embrace
Of
Hostile expanse
Of the sleeping
Earth,
Sky, mountains, stars,
- All sleeping
Happily

I,
A microcosm
Grope my way
To nowhere.

Nature
In
Silent
Solitude,
Tranquil
&
Dreaming.
Not I .

- Indira Shah

Jayantilal V. Sheth

2 Appleby Lane, East Brunswick, NJ 08816; he loves writing poems and spiritual songs in Gujarati and English; science graduate; retired Executive of Unichem Laboratories Ltd. Bombay; social worker.

IT IS A SPRING TIME

It is a spring time.
Throw your coats and sweaters,
Enjoy the beautiful weather.
The chicks that chuckle the sparrows that flutter.
Green leaves cover the trees,
The buds that sprout and smile.
The beautiful flowers,
They want to talk about the past showers.
The sky is bright, the men in delight,
There is a song on the lips of lovers.
It is a spring time, It is a spring time.

- Jayantilal V. Sheth

IDENTITY

Man seized behind
The barbed wire
At a regroupment center
Was not an ally
Or enemy.

He was just a father
Holding his son so close to his heart
Comforting him
Under the blazing sun
And pointed guns.

- Kalpana Singh-Chitnis

SIMPLY A WITNESS

Storms in the desert roar
As you pray in a disatant land
Before the first bullet comes out
From your triumphant guns.

Humans are defined as
Flesh and blood
Once again,
As the pages of history turn.

I'm not here to decide that
A war is just or unjust

I'm "TIME"
Simply
A witness.

— *Kalpana Singh-Chitnis*

FRIENDS

Friends are they

> Who are always dear

No matter how far

> They are always near

At the time of sorrow

> They come with tear

At the time of happiness

> They jump and cheer

At the time of depression

> They break your fear

At the time of suppression

> They change your gear

In poverty or wealth

> Their minds are clear

Friends are they

> Who are always dear.

- Kundan Patel

ON YOUR BIRTHDAY

On your Birthday, you must be getting lots of greetings
Reminding you to have lots of fun, to let you know
How much they love you, are proud of you and care for you.

All that is well meant and well said.
However, I am not going to do any of those things today.
Because I include them in my prayer each and everyday.

I want to say things that are seldom said. To look back and
correct the course. Understand and stay focused on life's
priorities, considering future security and happiness.

To understand your capabilities and means.
Have high expectation but take one stride at a time
Rather than to loose out on life.

Take time off to enjoy little things like feeling the breeze,
Smelling the roses or playing with puppy rather than
Waiting for big things to happen.

Thank God that you are highly privileged.
Think of millions who could not be fortunate enough
In spite of all the efforts and hard work.

So on this day touch someone underprivileged,
Unfortunate or one who is left behind in life.

WISH YOU A VERY HAPPY BIRTHDAY.

- Laxmi S. Chowdhury

Monika Y. Chokshi

She has written English poems since her childhood. She likes reading English literature, Cultural dancing. She likes playing Indian & American songs on the piano. She did her B.S. in Computer science from Rutgers Univ. where she was the member of Golden key International Honor Society and was honored by The National society of Collegiate Scholars. She has been working with Merrill Lynch Company, NJ for the past two yrs. as part of the Technology Leadership program. She is also taking courses at the Wharton Institute of Management, Univ. of Penn. and planning to do her MBA. There is human side of her activities: she is the web master of "Asha for Eduction" a non-profit organization raising money to educate underpreviledged children in India and mentors a child at an elementary school. She knows Spanish and speaks fluent Gujarati although a US born citizen.

To our parents on their 25th wedding Anniversary

It has been 25 years
And we want to thank you for it all
You've always been there to take away our tears
And more importantly you've showed us
How to be confident and stand tall.

You've made us into who we are today
And never limited what we could be
Your love and support every step of the way
Is truly appreciated by both Moulin and me.

Your lives have truly shown us the way
We have learned from you how to act, live and pray
In our hearts we will always know
That no matter where we are, we'll never be alone.

Your guiding light and assistance
Has enabled us to go the distance.
Through your lives we have learnt courage and inspiration
And we only hope we can match your dedication.

We want to thank you for the memories we have shared
And let you know how much we've cared.
We have truly cherished the moments we have had
No one is more important to us than you, mom and dad.

We appreciate what you have done
From keeping us company to having fun.
We are grateful for your advice that has kept us focused and
strong without your help we would not be who we are today
or have lasted as long.

As parents, mentors and friends you have always been there
No one else in our life can even compare.
As our lives have slowly progressed
We have realized how we are truly blessed.

You have taught us more than you will ever know
From your example we have changed and continue to grow.
Our only hope is that you are proud and content. For that
Reason we celebrate your marriage on this joyous event.

- *Monika Y. Chokshi* (*Together with brother Moulin*)

Moulin Y. Chokshi

He writes poems and articles, since he was in middle school ; his Writings have appeared in some magazines including his High School's News paper "Hawkeye" ; he is 18 yrs. age and presently studying at The Northwestern university, Illinois in The seven Years M.D. program; achieved The National Merit Scholarship; As the editor of his High School's Newspaper 'Hawkeye', he interviewed many distinguished personalities, including environmentalists fighting for the preservation of historical areas and The UN representative from Zimbabwe; he is the past-vice president of "The Social Studies Forum". He is the recipient of · The NJ Governor's School of Eng. and Tech. Scholar Award, The John Hopkins University's Talent Search Award and Lad Vanik samaj of N.A. Achievement Award: He volunteered his services at Muhlenberg Hospital and First Aid squad in New Jersey: He loves playing saxophone and piano and performed in Marching band.

NEW YEAR'S DAY

On the night of New Year's Day,
The children anxiously began to pray
For what would be a marvelous wonder.
They looked up into the sky,
Never blinking an eye
Waiting for a cloud or some thunder.

The hours quickly passed with no end effect
A sense of gloom in the students one could detect.
One could hear a muffled groan
As they thought of School, and let out a petulant moan.
Slowly, but surely every last child went to bed.

Overwhelmed by what could only be described as a deep sense of dread.
What miracle did these children restlessly foresee?
What did they pray for, but to no avail?
What marvel did not seem to prevail?
Snow, is what they wanted, at least an inch, or maybe three.

During the night, when all were asleep,
Snow began to fall, two feet deep.
White could be seen as far as the eye could see,
But would the children have a "No school" decree?

One by one, they awoke to a surprise,
Their joyous phenomenon came from the skies
It was a beautiful sight, untouched and pure snow
On the trees, the rooftops, and the grass
A vision of simplicity nothing could surpass,
Nature at its apex, of wintry glow.

But all was not final, would there be school?
Would school continue; could the board be so cruel?
The Children impatiently waited for those three words,
They listened to the radio, waiting for it to be heard.

The broadcaster did not mention a school closing or delay,
Until finally those three golden words were said,
"No school today".
The children went into a state of commotion.
The unbelievable had come to pass,
They had a free day without a class.
It would be a day of joy and emotion.
Armed with sleds and boots,
 And mittens and winter suits,
The children rushed out to enjoy their day.
Snowballs were thrown and snow angles were made,
Strangers and friends alike played.
But nothing could match the speed of a ride
On a dog sleigh.

The exhilaration of the sled, which nothing could surpass,
They raced for hours at high speeds, no one wanted to be last.
Only the warm breaks of hot cocoa, could tear the children away
From their long awaited propitious day.

Unfortunately, the sun began to set, and its rays faded,
The students wanted to stay;
They said, they would never get jaded.
In a familiar pattern, the adolescents reluctantly got out of
their sleds.
The snow had almost melted after a day of relative heat,
And so dissolved the astounding treat,
But the fond memories would not dissipate from their heads.

The young children slowly trudged away from the snow,
After a day of enjoyment, their day ended in woe.
Why were the children so despondent and filled with despair?
What did they remember that made them fearfully swear?

In their warm cozy little cots,
Not a single child forgot,
That a fully day of school was ahead.
Amid groans and moans of self pity,
Praying for a plan to avoid the school of the city
And looking at the next day with a sense of dread.
Again the depression of the children began to set in,
They walked disconsolately around the house,
Never bearing a grin.
Just as they waited the night before.
They stayed up waiting for something to happen,
Until they could no more.

On the night after New Year's Day,
The children again began to pray
For what would be a marvelous wonder.
They looked up into the sky,
Never blinking an eye
Would they get a cloud or thunder?

- *Moulin Chokshi*

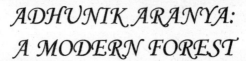

ADHUNIK ARANYA: A MODERN FOREST

Fierce creatures – humans – roam this forest

Made of concrete, stone, cement and glass.

An iron rainbow drops down from the sky.

Vegetation? No creepers trail, no tall trees sway;

Radios chirp full blast, but no birds fly.

An asphalt road, but stream, here unwinds.

No ghosts, but strange buildings rear their sides.

No fairies here but moving cars and trams.

Have hell's exhalations, molten sighs,

Risen, cooled, set and frozen here?

Or did a demon's scattered dreadful dreams

Sprout, flower and fruit in these enormous forms?

Forest? A mirage ! Mystery! On his solitary rounds

Did Purandar himself here lose his way?

– *Niranjan Bhagat*

BLIND MAN

Am I still to emerge from the womb?
How long, how long?
The flames have died on the funeral pyre,
And do I not live in my own body ?
Did he look in error into these eyes,
And was that why my light was suddenly quenched?
They spoke so much in heaven about this world
That I came in a hurry, leaving my eyes behind
In the shade of the kalpavriksha tree.
I'd dream I'd see the beauty of the earth,
But now even the blazing sun would fail as glasses!
I have no desire to lift my head
To heaven, sliding from one darkness to another.
Who says sun, moon and stars are lit?
They only shake a moment in the darkness.
I have discovered the world's secret:
In the heart of light lives darkness.
Don't take me to be philosopher, sleepwalker.
Oh you, say nothing. Don't dwell in blindness
All you who call me blind !

- Niranjan Bhagat

HOMESICKNESS

Uprooting a flower tree
From faraway tropical Bombay
I replanted it
In this cold alien Philadelphia
And determined that
I would see to its survival.
Yet
When the spring here spews cherry blossom pink
I crave for saffron kesuda flowers.
When the whole earth here erupts hot summer roses
My eyes cry red for Gulmohar.
It rains here all twelve months
Yet
The monsoon fragrance of India
Never ever leaves me free.
We have everything here
And yet nothing.

I am homesick.
Feel like
Packing my bags
And going home…

But where is my home ?

— *Panna Naik*

THE LIVING ROOM

I reorganize my living room

Asking each piece

Where it would like to be placed.

I give a new spot to the sofa and the lamp,

Change the drapes, and

Replace the old rug with a wall-to-wall carpet.

The living room with its new decor

Looks precise and proper.

When everything is thus in place

I begin to wonder!

Where among these things

Should I place myself ?

- Panna Naik

MISS ME, BUT LET ME GO

When I come to the end of the road,
And the sun has set for me.
I want no rites in gloom filled room,
Why cry for a soul set free?

Miss me a little, but not too long,
And not with your head bowed low
Remember the love that we once shared.

Miss me, but let me go,
For this is a journey, we all must take
and each must go alone.
It's all part of master's plan,
a step on the road to home.

When you are lonely and sick at heart,
go to the friends we know.
And bury your sorrows in good deeds,
Miss me but let me go.

                              - *Pravin Patel [Shashi]*

FIREFIGHTER'S PRAYER

When I am called to duty,
Wherever flames may rage,
Give me the strength to save a life
Whatever be its age.

Help me embrace a little child
Before it is too late,
Or save an older person from
The horror of that fate.

Enable me to be alert
And hear the weakest shout,
And quickly and efficiently
To put the fire out.

I want to fill my calling and
To give the best in me,
To guard my every neighbor and
Protect his property.

And if according to God's will
I must answer death's call,
Bless with your protecting hand,
My family one and all.

- *Pravin Patel [Shashi]*

POSSESSING *CHOMOLUNGMA

Awed and blessed at once
I forget to blink -
As if the mountain will move away.
It has risen to claim the sky completely,
The tallest vision in the world.
And yet, I dare to confess
My heart seems to soar higher.
It is close to me-massive;
I am close to it-submissive.
Face after face is revealed,
Most overlapping folds
Are flung open.
We see what truely is
My breath is taken away,
And I am most alive.
I stretch my arms,
And my desire is fulfilled.
The body of the soul melts
Like snow in summer.
Rivers flow
Bearing reflections
of the High priest -
The sharp peak above,
The one that is mine,
mine own,
mine alone.

*The name for Everest in Tibetan language.

— *Preety Sengupta*

ALAS !

He asked,
"Are you glad I called?"
"Oh ya", she said.
He said something,
She said something.
Who was listening?
Minutes passed.
Was it a bad connection?
"So what else is new?"
He asked.
"This" and "That"
"I am glad you are home",
He said.
"Oh ya", she said.
"So what else is happening?"
He asked.
It did seem like a bad connection.
"What did you say?"
"Did you say something?" –
Nothing was said, or understood.
"So what else?"
     "What else?"
He kept asking.
She regretted being at home.

- *Preety Sengupta*

Rahi Karnik

34645 Winslow Ter., Fremont, CA 94555; she is Chemical Engineer and has graduated from univ. of California at Berkeley; she writes poems since her freshman college year; she worked as Ameri Core volunteer at Ground Zero in October 2001 for a month; she does Yoga, Rock-climbing, photography and plays santoor.

SANTOOR ABOUND

Echo into the
Hypnotic spell of walnut
Curved on prancing steel

Might crescendos
Tossing ears in a tailspin
Leaving triple trails

Of decrescendos
Whispering in a sustained
Tremor of squinty swings

Our eyes lock, as one
You, in your world of drum, me
In my world of strum

A pact unspoken
Offering sound to surround
The listener's heart

Santoor abound

- *Rahi Karnik*

IMAGINATION

Somewhere far away
There's little imagination
And it creates magnificent things
Without much thought.

As it elevates the crispy leaves
Embracing them with compassion
They are stitched back together
To attain that color.

As it tosses the chills
With a delicate rhythm
Everything is covered
To attain that color.

As it turns up the lights
Illuminating with grace
Sparks fly above
To attain that color.

And before it launches the moon tonight
To set the night afire
It will draw you two close together
To attain that color.

Perhaps this little imagination
That creates these wonderful things
Does not linger that far away
In an unfathomable dream.

While ecstasy captures the day
This little imagination
Lies so very close to you
For I have just given it away.

- Rahi Karnik

WRINKLES OF TIME

The wind stops to caress a strand of hair across my forehead,
Your thin weary fingers move to caress it aside.
You see my forehead wrinkled with time.

I saw you reading my thoughts across my forehead.
I saw you mocking my benign thoughts,
With your gleaming eyes.

The rites of passage,
Still write something on my forehead,
Some hold the mirth in those lines,
Some sit quietly by my side,
And when you smooth those lines with thin weary fingers,
Some gather me in their embrace,
Some long for a longing in your eyes,
And,
Then the world seems just a tiny speck in time.

- *Rajni Bhargava*

IT'S FALL....

It's fall and all is bare,
cool wind sometimes whips through the air,
then I thought of you,
some touched me, some were deep,
some were sad like fallen leaves,

Kids are playing happy and wild,
their thoughts are not like mine,
then I thought of you,
some were happy, some were wise,
some were free like a song in the wild.

- *Rajni Bhargava*

A MATURE LOVE

I love you………Keep this mirror
You love me……..I swear without horror
We vowed again and again
Sun or rain, artery or vein
To opening skies
In mirth and sighs
Echoes reverberate
Beyond time and space
Self-perpetuating ripples
Not by biniary fission,
Return happily within
Intertwining, enmeshing
Melting to solidify
The base of their bonfire
The Sun of our desire.

Torrents now leveled with time
Emotional volcanoes coiled in rhyme
Muddy waters settled to wade
Reflecting the bottomless bed
About which we never spoke
Our ignorance we never broke
How far the words can fly
When there is a limited sky !
Sparkling gold is sprinkled all over
In the rocks and sands of river
You must have an eye of achiever.

Now it is an amalgamated fathom

With realities of worldly wisdom

To coin the currency of love

So called self respect, bruising

The fingers that are cruising

A promise through turmoils,

Edging to Ego, everything foils.

A drop of blood, a pampered scream

Un expected pain, a central theme

Is the proof of living

For my pension purpose presented

To authority year by year, for believing.

We present the same proof of being alive

To each other every moment, so naïve.

Everything seems to be in place, tranquil.

A reality of life, a new equation, refill,

To be in pain means in love.

- Dr. Rasik Pandya

FAN !!

I landed in Maryland when I came
I started watching Orioles game
I did not know the game then
Nor the team, but became a fan.

I followed Orioles wherever they played
Win or lose, was not at all swayed.
Then I moved from state to state
Orioles did not remain that first rate.

I started loving the play and players
For any one were not my prayers
I thought it was quite rational
To become objective and professional.

But was it right to stay rational
About something so personal or national ?

- Dr. Rasik Pandya

POETRY

Poetry is the deep emotions,
of my heart.
The depth of feelings,
in the form of rhyme.
The feelings of your heart,
You cannot tell anybody.
The feelings you can only
write on the paper,
Which is your best friend,
in this whole wide world
Which always consoles you,
And appreciates you as a human being.
Poetry gives solace
to a wounded heart,
With the loving imagination.
And sweet lullaby.
Life is a struggle,
Hard to survive.
The world is so cruel,
It's hard to stand by.
Poetry is the solace,
gives feeling of pride.
Poetry uplifts the spirits,
Which soars like an angel
With the wings of imagination
And begin to fly in the sky.

- Sarojini Sharma

BEAUTY

Beauty lies in the purity of the heart,

Not in the physical beauty.

Physical beauty is going to fade away

With the length of time.

The purity and goodness of heart

Is eternal.

The fragrance of goodness and purity

Rises high to reach in the Heaven near God.

Just like Christ and Gandhi, their fragrance

Of purity and goodness remain immortal

In the history of mankind.

Beauty lies in the vail of dawn when the sky

Becomes colorful with the radiant rays of

The sun and begin to shine and the birds to fly in the sky.

Beauty lies in thoughts of kindness and giving

Food to a hungry person.

Beauty lies in helping and giving love to

Each other, because we all are the children

Of the same God, so we should act in our life

With love and care and act divine.

- Sarojini Sharma

Shirish J. Shastri

1210, North Oaks Blvd. North Brunswick, NJ 08902. He is Engineer by profession & writes English poems since many years. He is the active member of the Academy.

PLENARY POOL

Who has not lost a loved one ?

A sibling, a cousin

A parent, a child

A friend, a neighbor

Someone who is close

We see them suffer and go

Peace unto them.

When disaster strikes

We feel sorry and sad

Innocent victims

Peace unto them.

The Higher Power calling

We slow down and mature

Plenary pool of grief

teach us more

to pray, help, and heal.

- Shirish J. Shastri

TRIBUTE

Serene in the evening
On a sunny day of August
Grey and cotton clouds
Treetops green lined.
Bird singing and stopping.
Nearby sounds of intermittent
Phone ringing, faucet running.

Colorful insects and flowers
Decorative beautiful
Silent moving.

Mind running clips on
Hours and days gone by.
Absorption of thought
Absorption of scenery
Two worlds one within
One without.
Slowly you wake up
Both are slipping into eternal past.

- Shirish J. Shastri

THE CHARGE OF THE FIRE BRIGADE

[With apologies to Lord Tennyson]

Ten floors or twenty floors
Or eighty floors upward;
Up into the tower of death
Dashed the three hundred.

Dust to the left of them
Debris to the right;
Slabs crashing, sounds thrashing
Darkness dense and tight.

There's not to reason why
There's not to pause or pry,
There's but to try and die
To save their fellow men.

How can their glory fade?
O the noble change they made.
Into a burning Hell, made in mirth,
By heaven seekers, here on earth.

Lord Krishna said, "Do your duty
And forget the rewards."
These men knew no krishna
But they did their duty
And craved no awards.

Lord Jesus said, "Love your fellow men!"
Yes, Let Hell be hammed
And Devil be damned
And terror condemned;
But love, love, love, your fellow men!

These men did not pause
To think of Krishna, Christ or cause;
But they sure did love enough
To die for their fellow men !

If you have feelings abundant,
Hold your tears redundant;
For these brave men fearless,
Your tribute should be tearless.

They asked for no honors
Nor craved for candles crude;
Their memory is eternal myrrh
In the sweet smell of sandalwood!

- *Subodh Shah.*

THE CAMEL

Once upon a time
In a zoo American,
Stood a Camel, strong but cynical.
He looked to his left, he looked to his right,
He found animals inimical
And he jumped in fright.

"Look at these brats!
Look at their limbs—
Crooked and curvy, bent and bumpy, icky crimps!
Beak of hawk and doggy tail
Horn of bull and tiger nail,
Each one, every one, absurd obstruction,
Weapon of Destruction!"
—— so the Camel said.

But the Frenchy Fox
His wisdom pronounced:
"Sire Dear,
Though you denounced
One limb crooked in every beast
Yours are twenty in every twist."

[Based on an old Indian poem]

- *Subodh Shah*

REMORSE

It hurts.....
When paper brings
The number 200-300
Or more slain Just numbers...
Where cast and creed...
Beguiling- religion
Played the jeopardy game....

Myraid mustangs-
Muster- the vigor
And hollow-pride
Drugged in frizzling
Innocent lives....
The rampage-crusade
Of reaching-the God
Is an act-icy cold....

The impudent
Religion-Janitors
In fall-the heart and soul
Of a mother-when
Radio-Announces-
A faint chill-kills -
The hollowed-eyed
In extenso-jeremiad.

- Dr. Sudarshan 'Priyadarshini'

MAGNOLIAS

When magnolias

Bloom….

Under the shadow

Of moon….

Sweet like sugar

Dreamy honey moon

Feel the touch-

Underneath…..

Silky and smooth

When magnolias bloom……

- Dr. Sudarshan 'Priyadarshini'

Tony Hwilka

30 Needlepoint Lane, Willingboro, NJ 08046; he writes poems in English since many years; his ability to translate life's experiences into kaleidoscopic, incredible mini journeys sets apart "Untamed Violets" his first collection of poem recently published; his poems appeared in many magazines; he is the vice President of "The New Jersey Poetry Society" and active member of the Indo-American Literary Academy; he was born in Carnegie, Penn. and for sometimes in his fifties, served in Korea for The United States Army; following his Army Discharge at Fort Dix, NJ, he went from operating a Gas station to owning "Hwilka's Foreign cars" Which included seven franchises; he is licensed in mortgage and financial services; upon retiring, he obtained Real Estate Licence and continued financial services.

SHARING WITH NATURE

If you 're quiet
You'll hear whispers
Through wind and leaf
Gossip spreading tree to tree

And
If you listen
Instead of speak
You'll learn the wisdom
Of living in peace

- Tony Hwilka

YESTERDAY'S MELODY

I lie on the side
Of the mountain
High above the valley
Where I was born
Crisp air nibbles my ears
Beams of sun
Sift through the branches

A mountain bear
Appears out of the brush
Stands on hind legs
I, in agitated fright
Blow my horn
Blow my horn-loud
Bear looks in puzzlement
He growls – then vanishes
Days gone by to yesteryears
Clouds now black
Black with misery
Melody from my horn has ceased
The bear cannot reason
The horn is in my hand

Until my body blows within the wind
Down the valley where I was born
My horn
Goes to the bear.

- *Tony Hwilka*

TOMORROW

Tomorrow I will go and meet my father.
We will sip some tea together,
sweet and hot, perhaps herbal,
The morning sun falling on him through the window
As he sits on his Victorian reclining chair,
The breeze blowing over the due-bejeweled mogras*,
The tiny tomtit tuning for the day.
There will be no time for Time,
Not the little time generally closed in a small watch.
There will be no engagements to keep,
No hurry and flurry.
He will capture the life he has lived,
And I will remember my childhood.
When a procession of familiar faces would enter,
Mother would come and stand silently.
The replies to my eager questions
Even the sun would stop to listen.

This will happen tomorrow.

[*Mogras = Flowers of Mogra Plant]

- Viraf Kapadia

When claimants were Asked For a Place
In the Hall of fame Consecrated to Heroism
Both the Tears And the Fist Came Quarreling

The fist exclaimed

That it rose before

All weapons on the ground,

And history was made

And tears only showed

The ineffectual anger,

And what else?

Did sobbing ever move anything?

Tears could never stop

The fast whipping hand of the tyrant.

Every blow returned

Was a blow given

By a hand whose every joint

Was well oiled by tears.

- Viraf Kapadia

Alisha Mehndiratta

C/o Rajan Mehndiratta, 10 Madison Drive, Plainsboro; NJ 08536;
student of 5th grade, age 11, writes poems, enjoys free writing in
her Creative Writing Class; loves reading; plays piano, takes piano
classes since 4 years.

CHANGES OF LIFE

Leisurely slouching
                    on the most
                                comfy
                                    looking
                                        couch,
                    ever seen....
Reading by the
                            genuine sunlight- not aware,
that after only
            a
                few
                    more
                        years
                            to come,
she will
        not get
                    a single moment for herself.....
Hurrying,
        scurrying,
                    worrying too,
about others,
about family,
            but not,
                    about herself...
            MY MOTHER !!!
                            - Alisha Mehndiratta

Anuj Mehndiratta

C/o Rajan Mehndiratta, 10 Madison Dr., Planisboro, NJ 08536; student of 3rd grade, age 8 ; writes poems sometimes; mathematics is his favorite class; penguin is his favorite animal.

MY DAD

Jolly, solemn, hardworking.
Never ready to leave work in middle,
That's my dad
I feel proud of being proud of what he does
I feel safe when he's around
When he's near I've no fear.
Never close to crying
Surprising me all the time.

Dad, soft cushy, bouncy too,
I jump on him like mad.
He has a special thing in him-a very special spark,
A spark that makes him MY dad and NOBODY else's!!!

- *Anuj Mehndiratta*

A BRIGHT SIGHT

Light, quite bright in the night

Almost right

One twitch of a switch

Makes it very nice

What a sight of light

Hanging so tight

What a nice sight of light

Like a mini sun in my sight

I like that….

White

Sight of

light!

- *Anuj Mehndiratta*

Dwija Vaidya

105 Fornelius Ave. Clifton, NJ 07013; she loves writing poems in English; she is 9 yrs., third grade student.

THE MATH SANTA

One plus one equals two, the Math Santa told me too.

One plus two equals three, the Math Santa said I'm free.

One plus three equals four, the Math Santa took me on a tour.

One plus four equals five, the Math Santa taught me how to dive.

One plus five equals six, the Math Santa gave me the math game "PICK UP STIX".

One plus six equals seven, the Math Santa taught me how to count to eleven.

One plus seven equals eight, the Math Santa ate and ate.

One plus eight equals nine, the Math Santa said I'm fine.

One plus nine equals ten, the Math Santa told me to start again.

- Dwija Vaidya

Parth P. Desai

6411 Noble Rock Ct., Clifton, VA 20124; born in USA, 8 yrs. age, presently studying in 2nd grade, but wrote this poem at 6 yrs. age; enjoys drawing, coloring, writing stories, sometimes poems too; plays western music on violin and sometime plays Indian movie songs too; his favourite sports are basketball, baseball, soccer; participates in Boy scout activities; loves playing to visit places, beaches, other countries and museums; loves playing with his younger brother prashant and his grand parents. He stood first in Virginia State Chinmay Mission's Bal-Vihar's Geeta (Sanskrit) competition.

HELICOPTER

A helicopter in the sky
In the clouds, a helicopter goes,
This way and that
Goes even where up to my toes,
A helicopter is a plane
That everyone knows.

- Parth P. Desai

Vaibhavi Bhavsar

19 Lindsey Ct. Franklin park, NJ 08823; she loves writing poems in English; she is a 7th Grader; her interests are dancing and reading; she has attended higher level course at The Kalanjali School of Dance; she likes to do water color painting; she participated in teaching handicapped students. She is the winner of many awards, including National Award for English.

ALWAYS THERE

Always there,
To keep you company
When you're all alone.
To solve your problems
When you've found no solution.
To cheer you up
When you're down in the dumps.

Always there
To cheer you on,
When there's nobody in the stands.
To pick you up,
When you fall.
To stop you from doing things
You know you'll regret.

Always there,
When all you need
Is a little love.
When you've got
Nobody to turn to.
To remind you
When you've forgotten.

Always there
In your heart
To stay and to never go away.

So remember,
your family
Is
ALWAYS THERE.

- Vaibhavi Bhavsar

INDO-AMERICAN LITERARY ACADEMY'S

ANTHOLOGY OF POEMS (2005)

हिन्दी विभाग

Dr. Anjana Sandhir

*P.O.Box 1895, Canal Street Station, NY 10013; living in USA since 199::
eminent poet writing in Hindi, Urdu and Gujarati; published 8 collections c
poems and one thesis and edited 3 poetry collections. She contributed to the A
India Radio programs, TV serials; teaches Hindi through RBC Radio, participate
in various national and international Poetry-Reading Programs (Kavi-Sammelan
recipient of three Awards from The Gujarat Urdu Sahitya Academy and Gujara
Hindi Sahitya Academy; honoured by the mayor of Jersey City in The Gujara
Foundation's Kavi-Sammelan; she is professor of Hindi at The Columbi
University, New York; she also taught Hindi at Princeton University, NJ.*

बरसात गुजर गई

तकते - तकते राह तेरी बरसात गुजर गई सजना,
सोने जैसे दिन, चाँदी सी रात गुजर गई सजना ।
दूर दूर दीपक जलते हैं, दिल में जले अंधेरा,
कैसे मीठे सपनों की बारात गुजर गई सजना ।
तू भी मुझको याद करे वो दिन थे कितने प्यारे,
खुशियों के वो दिन, फूलों की बात गुजर गई सजना ।
बागों में झूले हँसते हैं, बाजारों में खुशियाँ,
अपनी तो वो खुशी जो तेरे साथ गुजर गई सजना ।
किस बैरन ने रोका तुझको , कहाँ किया विश्राम,
भीड़ भरी दुनिया की हर सौगात गुजर गई सजना ।
त्यौहारों के दिन भी हमने तेरी राह तकी है,
सुबह हुई,दोपहर हुई, फिर रात गुजर गई सजना ।
खेतों ने पोशाक पहन ली, पेड़ हुए हैं धानी,
तेरा दिल न बदला और बरसात गुजर गई सजना ।

- अंजना संधीर

चौराहे की लालबत्ती और ये तीन औरतें

स्कूल में बच्चों को छोड़ने आती
तीन दिशाओं से ये तीन औरतें
बच्चों को छोड़, हर रोज, खड़ी रहती हैं चौराहे के एक तरफ ।
करती रहती हैं बातें अपने सुख-दु:ख की ।
सरहदों की सीमाओं से दूर,
मुल्कों की राजनीति से बेखबर,
कारें, बसें आती, जाती हैं , सिग्नल की बत्तियाँ लाल
पीली, हरी होती रहती हैं,
बच्चों को छोड़ स्कूल में लोग जाते हैं, कुछ आते हैं
भीड़ छँट जाती है, धीरे-धीरे
दौड़ा-दौड़ी भी हो जाती है कम ।
मगर ये तीन औरतें ऐसे ही खड़ी रहती हैं
बारिश हो तो छाते लिए ,
ठण्ड में लम्बे कोट, सिर पे टोपियाँ, गले में
मफलर, हाथों में दस्ताने पहने,
भयानक हिमपात भी इनकी मुलाकात में
डालता नहीं है खलल ।
सब गोरी, काली, स्पेनीश, दक्षिण ऐशियाई
बच्चों को छोड़ने आई माताएँ
इन्हें हेलो ! हाय ! कहती हैं ।
ये भी हँसती हैं, देती हैं उन्हें जवाब।
फिर बातों में लग जाती हैं ।
दीवाली आती है या आती है ईद
तो लाती है इसी चौराहे पर मिठाइयाँ
देती हैं
क्रिसमस के तोहफे

नये साल की दुआएँ
जन्म दिन या शादी की सालगिरह की शुभ कामनाएँ !
लाता है जब कोई भारत या पाकिस्तान से मिठाई
या कोई सौगात तो तीनों बाँटती हैं आपस में,
और कोसती हैं कभी अपने यहाँ होने को
करती रहती हैं अपने मुल्कों को याद
जहाँ आराम की जिंदगी जीती थीं ये ।
कभी कोसती हैं बर्फीले मौसम को
जो घर से बाहर भी निकलते नहीं देता,
या कोसती हैं पीठ पीछे बैठे रिश्तेदारों को
जो यहाँ भी चैन की साँस नहीं लेने देते ।
कभी कभी बातें करते-करते
तीनों आगे बाजार की दुकानों में चली जाती हैं ।
जरूरी सामान खरीद
धीरे-धीरे चल, फिर उस चौराहे से
बिछड़ती हैं तीन दिशाओं में चलती
कहती हैं तीनों- चोबीस घंटो में
ये बीस पच्चीस मिनीट ही अपने हैं
बात कर के मन हल्का हो जाता है-
समस्या हो तो हल निकल आता है-
वरना दो कमरे के घर में
दो-दो बच्चों और पति के अलावा
किस से बोलें ? किस के पास समय है
इन के दुःख सुख के लिए ?
ढूंढ़ लिया है इन्होंने
इस मशीनी देश में, काम के झमेलों में,
ठण्डे बर्फीले बातावरण के अकेलेपन में
अपने लिए जीने का रास्ता !

- अंजना संधीर

· Anoop Bhargava

16 Dickinson Ct. Plainsboro, NJ 08536; writing poetry is not an option, it just happens with him; he writes poems in Hindi since he was nine. He won several prizes at all India Cultural Festivals while he was in College. He is the director of International Hindi Association and Organzied Ten City Kavi-Sammelan tour for poet "Neeraj' in North America. He had his graduate studies at Birla Institite of Tech. and Science, Pilani and Indian Inst.of Tech., Delhi.He works as independent info.Tech.Consultant in New Jersey and lives in USA for the last 18 yrs. He has a distinguished collection of 200 Giga Byte Music "All that is Worth Listening".

तुम

तुम समन्दर का किनारा हो
मै एक प्यासी लहर की तरह
तुम्हें चूमने के लिये उठता हूँ
तुम तो चट्टान की तरह
वैसी ही खड़ी रहती हो
मैं ही हर बार तुम्हें
बस छू के लौट जाता हूँ !

देखो मान लो
कल रात
तुम मेरे सपनों मे आई थीं
वरना सुबह सुबह
मेरी आँखों की
नमी का मतलब
और क्या हो सकता है !

मैं सोते सोते
चौंक कर
उठ जाता हूँ,
तुम ने ज़रूर
कोई बुरा ख़्वाब
देखा होगा !

चलो अब
उठ जाओ
और जमाने को
अपने चेहरे की ज़रा सी
रोशनी दे दो
देखो सूरज खुद
तुम्हारी खिड़की पर
तुम से रोशनी
मांगने आया है।

- अनूप भार्गव

(चार मुक्तक - तुम्हारे लिये)

तृप्ति का अहसास तुम हो
बिन बुझी सी प्यास तुम हो
मौत का कारण बनोगी
ज़िन्दगी की आस तुम हो ।

प्रणय की प्रेरणा तुम हो
विरह की वेदना तुम हो
निगाहों में तुम्हीं तुम हो
समय की चेतना तुम हो ।

सपनों का अध्याय तुम्हीं हो
फूलों का पर्याय तुम्हीं हो
एक पंक्ति में अगर कहूँ तो
जीवन का अभिप्राय तुम्हीं हो ।

सुख दुख की हर आशा तुम हो
चुम्बन की अभिलाषा तुम हो
मौत के आगे जाने क्या हो
जीवन की परिभाषा तुम हो ।

- अनूप भार्गव

Anuradha Amlekar

2515 Fourth Ave. Apt. 1203, Seattle, WA 98121; she writes poems in Marathi & Hindi since many years; after living for 28 yrs. in Canada, she lives in USA for the last 8 yrs.; music and literature are her favourite activities.

'फासला'

चंद गर्म साँसे कुछ सुलगती आहें
दिल क्या है अेक धुएँ का गोला ।

कुछ पिघलता लहू कुछ टपकती बूँदे
ज़िस्म क्या है, अेक मोम की ज्वाला ।

कुछ जलते पल, कुछ तपती यादें
जिन्दगी क्या है, बुझतासा शोला ।

दिन ये कि उमड़ते घुमड़ते तूफान,
बरसते धुँआधार, खुशियों का ढेला ।

उमर थी कि पानी का रेला
रंगीला मौसम, लहराता झूला ।

अरमान थे कि सफेद, छितरे बादल
उड़ती पवन, रंगो का खेला ।

अेक तार था जोड़े हुअे दोनों की शृंखला
ये समय का जाला, बन गया है फासला ।

– अनुराधा आमलेकर

प्रियतम

तुम मेरे अशांत मनको, शांति का सन्मार्ग दिखा दो।
जलती हुई दिल की अगनपर, स्नेहजल की धारा बरसादो।
तुम ही सिखलादो मुझको ये, कैसे जीना आँसू पीकर,
मेरा गीत तुम्हारा ही है, तुम अपना स्वर इसको दे दो।

तुम ही तो हो मेरी कल्पना, तुम्हारी ही कविता गाऊँगी,
यथार्थ के काँटोंपे चलकर, तुम्हें फूल मैं बना रखूँगी,
कबसे मुझको थी ये तलाश, तुम जाने कहाँ छुपे थे,
आज अचानक ऐसे आये, जैसे सदियों अंतरमें थे।

तुम ही बनो मेरा सहारा, तुम बिन कैसे जीवन मेरा,
तुमको छुपाकर मनमें अपने, दुःख लुटादूँ अपना सारा,
मुझमें ऐसी शक्ति भरदो, दुनियाँ के सब गम भूला दो,
मेरे अद्भुत ख़्वाबों को तुम, सपनों ही से पूरा कर दो।

दुनियाँ से अब कुछ न कहूँगी, जो कहना तुमको कह दूँगी,
तुमको पाकर, तुममें खोकर, मेरा जीवन सँवार लूँगी,
तुम न हो तो अनगिनत ये, बोझ मैं कैसे उठा सकूँगी,
साथ तुम्हारे चलते चलते, सारा यौवन गुजार दूँगी।

तुम न कभी अब जाना प्रियतम, वादा करना मुझसे अबही,
जब मेरा मन उदास होगा मनमें आना फौरन तबही,
गही जिंदगी में बाकी है, वरना हो जायेगी तबाही,
घुट घुट के फिर मौत कटेगी, मैंने उससे वफा निबाही।

- अनुराधा आमलेकर

इंडो-अमेरिकन राष्ट्रगीत

भारत अमेरिका है प्यारे वतन हमारे।
दोनों की हिफाजत से दुरस्त है तन हमारे।

दोनों के उपवनों में बहती हवा वही है,
साँसों में वही हवा ले, चलते जीवन हमारे।

चिट्ठी न हो वतन से बढ़ती है दिल की धड़कन
करते है फोन फौरन प्यारे स्वजन हमारे।

दु:खी हो अपने जब जब बिलकुल पिघलता है दिल,
आँसु से छलक जाते दोनों नयन हमारे।

मिलते हमें जो डोलर, सब चाहिए न हमको
रुपयों में गिन वतनको भेजत हैं धन हमारे।

दोनोंकी अच्छी बातें बच्चों को हम बताते
ऐसी है परवरिश और ऐसे जतन हमारे।

पंछी भी कभी उड़ कर आते यहाँ वतन से
स्वागत के लिये उनके खुले सदन हमारे।

दोनोंकी तरक्की और दोस्ती के लिये सबकुछ
करते हम मर मिटेंगे, ऐसे स्वपन हमारे।

दोनों हमारी माता, दोनोंको लाख वंदन
करने को उनकी पूजा खिलते सुमन हमारे।

दोनों को चाहते हम फिर भी जगह है दिल में
दुनिया को चाहने को बेचैन मन हमारे।

— चंद्रकान्त देसाई

आँखमिचोली

खेलत राधा आँखमिचोली
मौन अधरसे उठत मधुरी
अगमनिगमकी बोली।....खेलत.
गोकुलसे दूर भाग श्याम अब द्वारिका में बसत है,
बंसी बजती अब ना मधुबन, घटघट श्याम घूमत है,
राधाअंतर नाचत थनगन
नहीं ढोल नहीं ढोली।....खेलत.
राधा की चुनरीके रंग हैं पलपल पलटे जावत,
कभी मेघधनु, मोरपिच्छ कभी, श्याम श्याम कभी होवत,
अंदर बाहर रंगरंग बस
राधा खेलत होली।....खेलत.
वृंदावन से अलकमलक की हवा शीतल है आवत,
पल्लव पल्लव मधुमय बोलत, कौन अकल गीत गावत ?
सूर बजत बिन साज हृदय में
राधा डगमग डोली।....खेलत.
जीवनबंसरी मधुर बजावत, स्वयं क्हान भई राधा,
प्रीतपवनको भर बंसीमें रेलत सूर अगाधा,
स्वर्गअप्सरा शरमा गई सुन
सूरकी झलक अमोली।....खेलत.
राधा की अँखियन में जगमग ज्योति होत अनुपम,
रैनमें देखत चाँद पूनमका, विरह व्यथा में संगम,
श्यामविहीन मधुबन में खेले
रास राधिका गोरी।......खेलत.

- चंद्रकान्त देसाई

Dr. Dhananjaya Kumar

7806 Wendy Ridge Lane, Annandale, VA 22003: he writes poetry in Hindi and English; he is a writer, actor, producer, director, teacher of music, Yoga and meditation, script-writer, script-advisor, composer of music of songs and ghazals and an Economist; published two collections of Hindi poems; his Hindi poems published in several literary magazines and Anthologies;English poems published in American poetry Anthology; English songs published by Hilltop Records in "Best of Country Songs in American" ;Hindi and English poetry recitals in several TV programs; presenter and panelist of Hindi diaspora literature at Yale University (2004); recipient of Hindi Literary Awards: Sahitya Sarswat (Gujarat) and Shaan-e-Adab(Madhya Pradesh); lives in USA for the last 35 years; he is M.A.(Economics) from Harvard University and Ph.D.(Economics) from George Washington University; receeipient of several English poetry awards by International Society of Poets;edited, complied and published book of over 1000 inspirational passages from the great minds of the East and West(2004); Author of the major reform proposal "Drive to overcome violence through Eduction" Authored or co-authored numerous books and other publications by The World bank, from where retired as Senior Industrial Economist in 1998 after 25 yrs. of service spanning various countries; composed & directed music & staged numerous plays on TV programs; perfomed music for many CDs & videos and directed Jhankar music group;conducted seminars and workshops on Indian classical music, Yoga, meditation and Yoga-therapy in USA; appeared as guest-speaker on several TV talk shows; chaired several sessions at The World Vedic Conference in Wash.D.C.(2004); written, produced & directed 70 video programs on healing yoga for various ailments;awarded "Yogacharya" and "Professor of yoga" by International Yoga Federation & appointed as its director; vice-president of International Yoga Therapy & Ayurveda

Association; Founder & Director of India International school in USA, teaching classes in music, yoga & meditation; performed multi-lingual dubbing for discovery channel programs.

गजल

मौज, साहिल, या सफ़ीने का सहारा हो, न हो
हम नदी का जोश देखेंगे, किनारा हो, न हो

आशिक़ों के नाम है तक्सीम मेरी ज़िन्दगी
बाद मरने के कोई हिस्सा हमारा हो, न हो

मैं इक्कठा कर रहा हूँ कतरा कतरा प्यार का
संगदिल की रहनुमाई में गुजारा हो, न हो

आखिरी मौका है शायद, अब मुहब्बत कर ही लूँ
ज़िन्दगी से क्या पता मिलना दोबारा हो, न हो

उसकी बातें राख कर जायेंगी मुझको एक दिन
मुझको ठण्डा कर सके ऐसा इशारा हो, न हो

दिलको जो बहलायेगी वो राह तुम्हारी हो, न हो
यार मिल भी जाये तो मिलकर हमारा हो, न हो

झूठ की कच्ची इमारत में हुई है परवरिश
क्या पता सच्चाई उनको गँवारा हो, न हो.

- धनंजय कुमार

अन्तिम किरण

आज   देखना   है
कहाँ ले जाती हैं मुझे
मेरे सोच की किरणें ?
एक किरण फूटती है
तो देखता हूँ अपना इतिहास
सबसे जुड़ा हुआ सा।
दूसरी किरण बन गई
इतिहास बदलने का प्रयास।
तीसरी किरण छिटकी है
ज्ञान के गर्द में छिपे
अज्ञान के पर्दे पर।
चौथी किरण ने सजाया है
सपनों का झिलमिल संसार।
पाँचवी किरण ने जताया
आकाश का अनन्त विस्तार।
छठ्ठी किरण समेट लाई
सोच के स्त्रोत बिन्दु पर,
और सातवी किरणने
उस बिन्दु को धोकर बहा दिया।
अब न मैं हू, न प्रकाश,
शून्य में विलीन है
कुछ न होने का एहसास।

– धनंजय कुमार

Dr. Govardhan Sharma

837 Bluestone Lane, Bridgewater, NJ 08807. He is the Eminent Hindi writer in fiction, non-fiction and poetry and author of over 50 books in Hindi. He is the distinguished award winner from many states Literary Academies including those of Uttar Pradesh, Madhya Pradesh, Rajasthan and Gujarat. He is Ph.D. in Hindi and Sahitya Vachaspati. He was professor and Head of The Hindi Dept. in many Govt. Colleges and retired as Principal of Science and Arts College, Gandhingar, India. He is the author in Gujarati and Rajasthani languages in addition to Hindi. He has done extensive research on "Kachchhi" and published 11 books on the language and culture of Kachchhi people.

देखले हिमपात साथी !

बीत चुकी आज रजनी,
क्या सजा यह साज सजनी.
ठंड के झोंके पवन के, आज कैसा प्रातः साथी !

जगत धारे श्वेत बाना.
गा न सकते आज गाना,
कंठ है अवरुद्ध जब निज, राग गय कब गात राथी !

पेड़ पौधे और सब घर,
हिममय है आज तरुवर,
गल रहा है बर्फ भी अब हो रहा जलपात साथी !

दुःख उठाते हैं अनेकों,
पूछता मैं-आज रेखाओं
से मिले कुछ हाल भी निज, हो भविष्यत ज्ञात साथी !
पास में गहरा सरोवर,
छा गया हिम आज ऊपर,
ठंड ऐसी पा रहे हैं, कुछ न करते बात साथी !

हो यदि यह ठंड नित ही,
सृष्टि की हो जाये इति श्री,
यदि मिले हमेशा शाम या प्रभात साथी !

ठूंठ से दोनों खड़े अब,
हो गया है हाल बेढ़ब,
आ गया है आज पतझड़, गिर गये सब पात साथी!

देखले हिमपात साथी !

— गोवर्द्धन शर्मा

तुम मानो या न मानो

तुम मानो या न मानो,
यह जो लावारिस लाश पड़ी है,
मेरी ही है।
तब मैं मंदिर का सपूत था,
मस्जिद का फरजंद था,
चर्च, गुरुद्वारा, उपासरा,
अगियारी, देवद्वारा,
विहार, मठ, सिनेगोग और संतद्वारा-
सबका कुछ न कुछ था ।
मैं भ्रम में था-
कि सब मुझे अपना मानते हैं,
अपना आत्मीय कर जानते हैं ।
मैं इन सबका आधार था।
मैं इन सबका श्रृंगार था ।
पर आज सबने
अपना मानना तो दूर रहा,
पहचानने से भी इनकार कर दिया,

क्योंकि लाश पर शिनाख्त के लिए
कोई चिन्ह न था।
न कड़ा, न खतना, न चोटी और न.....
इसीलिए सबकी होते हुए भी,
सबके होते हुए भी,
यह लाश लावारिश पड़ी है।
तुम मानो या न मानो,
यह कफन बिना की लाश मेरी ही तो है।
राजनेता दुर्योधन ने
पूँजीपति दुःशासन से मिल,
मुझे निर्वस्त्र कर दिया है।
सामंती शकुनि का अनीतिमूलक दाव ही
इन्हें रास आया है।
'पराया माल अपना' का गुरुमंत्र ही
इन्हें मन भाया है।
सबने मिलकर मुझे कर दिया है नंगा,
और ये सब लोग
मेरे कफ़न के लिए दान की अपील करते हैं !
मारते हैं अनेक बेकसूर,
करवाते हैं दंगा,
ताकि कफ़न-लूट का इनका धंधा
चलता रहे ।
जुग-जुगों तक इनका राज फलता रहे !
यही क्या कम है,
कि उन्होंने विदेशी मुद्रा के लालच में
मेरा कंकाल निर्यात नहीं किया है।
जिस धरती का मैं जाया हूँ,
उस पर अभी तक
पड़े रहने दिया है !

— गोवर्द्धन शर्मा

Gulab Khandelwal

3477 Hunting Run Road, Medina, OH 44256; he writes since over 65 years; he writes poems including songs, doha, sonnets, rubai, ghazals, muktaks, prabandh poetry, poetic plays, mahakavya etc.; his 48 poetry-books and two plays have been published; his first book of poem was published in 1941; his writings have been edited and published by Narayan Chaturvedi in five volumes of "Gulab Granthavali"; he received Awards from Utter Pradesh Govt. and Bihar Govt. for his six books; he received Award from Hanuman mandir Trust for his poetry-book "Ahalya"; International Hindi Samiti honoured him as "A special/distinguished poet" in Wash.D.C. on Dec. 6, 1986, and the same day was declared by The Governor of Maryland State to be celebrated as "Hindi Language Day" he was awarded Honourary Citizenship of Baltimore City for his achievement in poetry; various universities have recognized his literature for the critical study for M.A. and Ph.D. students; his poem "Alokvrutt' is incorporated in the college text-book; he is the president of The All India Hindi Sahitya Sammelan for the last 10 years; he is the special member of the editorial committee of The American Tri-monthly "Vishwa" of The International Hindi Samiti; he is the top ranking poet of Hindi and lives in Ohio; Kumar Sabha of Calcutta honoured him as "Bhavonka Rajkumar" (Prince of poetic emotion).

बात जो....

बात जो कहने की थी होंठों पे लाकर रह गये ।
आपकी महफ़िल में हम ख़ामोश अक्सर रह गये ।
एक दिल की राह में आया था छोटा-सा मुकाम
हम उसीको प्यार की मंजिल समझकर रह गये ।
यों तो आने से रहे घर पर हमारे एक दिन
उम्र भर को वे हमारे दिल में आकर रह गये ।
फ़िक्र क्या अब तो नज़र आने लगा है उनका घर
बीच में बस मील के दो-चार पत्थर रह गये ।
कारवाँ गुजरे बहारों के भी सज-धजकर गुलाब
तुम हमेशा बाँधते ही अपना बिस्तर रह गये ।

– गुलाब खंडेलवाल

नाथ ! तुम जिसको अपना लेते

नाथ ! तुम जिसको अपना लेते
पहले तपा आग में उसको फिर कंचन कर देते!

पत्नी के न वचन चुभ जाते
क्या तुलसी तुलसी बन पाते !
धोखा यदि न प्रेम में खाते
योग भरथरी सेते !

मोहमुक्त करने को अंतर
तुम भक्तों को देते ठोकर
वही कृपा ही है जब मुझ पर
क्यों मन मूढ़ न चेते !

जिसका मन तुम में रम जाता
वह हित-हानि न चित में लाता
उर दो, पहुँचूँ तुम तक, दाता !
मैं भी नौका खेते!

नाथ ! तुम जिसको अपना लेते
पहले तपा आग में उसको फिर कंचन कर देते!

– *गुलाब खंडेलवाल*

Dr. Hemant Sharma

68 Maria Court, Kendall Park, NJ 08824; he writes Hindi poems since many years; he belongs to the family of writers, his father Dr. Govardhan Sharma is an Eminent Hindi writer & poet; he was intensely involved in the theatrical activities for 20 yrs. in India and foreign countries; he participated in Radio and TV programs; as Theatre-Artist, he was honoured by Triveni Lions Club and many other organizations; he possesses Ph.D. in Science and works as Analytical Chemist in Pharmaceutical's Quality Control Dept. in New Jersey; In India he worked as senior scientific officer at Gujarat Public Health Eng. Lab. and Guj. Jalseva Training Inst. Gandhinagar for many Years; he is a prominent active member of The Indo-American Literary Academy.

चार कवितायें

(९)

हर रोज
रात जब,
शाम की बैसाखीं के सहारे
मेरे आँगन में उतर आती है,
मौत धीमे से हाथ बढ़ा
मेरी हड्डियाँ टटोलने लगती है,
सदमों स्मृतियों के गिद्ध,
मेरा मांस नोंचने लगते हैं।
निराशा की जोंकें
मेरे रिसते लहू पर
रपटने लगती हैं।

असफलताओं के कीड़े
मेरी तमन्नाओं के बहते घावों में
कुलबुलाने लगते हैं,
और तब मैं
आत्महीनता की मक्खियों की,
भिनभिनाहट को भूल,
किसी फटे फटे वस्त्र वाले
सड़े सड़े कोढ़ी की तरह
अंगुली विहीन गला गला पंजा,
आँखों पर रख
करवट बदल लेता हूँ।

(२)

आस के बादल,
तेरे नभ पर
छितर छितर कर
रीते रीते।
सावन आया
आया सावन
शोर मचा,
दिन यूंही बीते।

बाहर खुश हैं,
भीतर गलते,
मुस्कानों में तेवर
पलते।
झूठ की फसलें

रोज ही ढ़ोते
काश कभी हम
सच भी बोते।

(३)

दीपावली
शायद मुझे
इसीलिये भाती है,
सोये शहरों पर
मुर्दा चेहरों पर
क्षणिक ही सही
रोशनी तो आती है !

(४)

कविता लिख
उसे जी न सकें तो
'थोथाचना'
कहलायें क्यों ?
वक्त सड़ा
मस्तिष्क लड़ाकर
कविता नई (!)
बनायें क्यों ?

– हेमन्त शर्मा

Himanshu Pathak

16 Cape May Drive, Marlboro, NJ 07746; he writes Hindi poems, short stories and articles since many years; he favours writing vyang poems projecting the discripencies of the society; his poems and writings have appeared in various magazines and anthologies; loves music and literature; he is Engineer by profession and lives in New Jersey since many years.

अमरीका में धाक जमा लो

अब अमरीका आहीगए तो जीवन का कुछ अर्थ बना लो।
साम दाम या दण्ड भेद से अमरीका में धाक जमा लो ॥

नई दिल्ली का लिखा पढ़ा पर राजा हूँ मैं बीकानेरी।
अपनी बात नहीं करता पर फाइव-स्टार चलती है मेरी।
गिनें-चुनें पूँजीपतियों के झट-पट से कुछ नाम गिना लो॥
अमरीका में धाक जमा लो ॥

मुम्बई का मैं सदा निवासी जुहू बीच पर मेरी कोठी।
अमिताभ, धर्में‍द्र, जीतु संग बांधा करता सदा लंगोटी।
दीना पाठक चाची जैसी बर्मन दा की बात चला लो॥
अमरीका में धाक जमा लो ॥

कवि नीरज का मैं हमजोली दिनकर के पिछवाड़े रहता।
व्यास मनोहर शैल संग मैं लाल किले से कविता करता।
कोई कब जाने क्या सच है ऊँची ऊँची बात बना लो॥
अमरीका में धाक जमा लो ॥

मैं स्वामी तिरछानन्द चेला शास्त्र के अस्त्र चला सकता हूँ ।
वाक्-देवी जब साथ न दें तो गेरूआ वस्त्र चढ़ा सकता हूँ ।
पढ़े लिखे सब हुए कुतर्की बहु अज्ञानी भक्त बना लो ।।
अमरीका में धाक जमा लो ।।

उपनिषद गीता घोंट रखे हैं, श्रीमद् भागवत का मैं ज्ञाता ।
रामायण करता पारायण कर्म कांड नित उदर निभाता ।
पत्नी तीनों जब भाग गई तो अब चौथी से ब्याह रचा लो ।।
अमरीका में धाक जमा लो ।।

महिलामंडल की मैं स्वामिनी, भारत की एक नारी निराली ।
पूर्वी हो या पश्चिम संस्कृति दोनों की ही बात निराली ।
तीन तलाक से हो सब हासिल ऐसा ही कुछ चक्र चला लो ।।
अमरीका में धाक जमा लो ।।

धर्मराज का सच्चा शिष्य हूँ, चौपड़ चलता चपल चाल से ।
धर्म-कर्म की बात उठे तो ध्वज फहराता उच्च भाल से ।
पर-धर्मों की बात चले यदि, घायल करता बड़े घाव से ।
धर्म नाम पर चन्दा ले कर, अपना स्विस बैलेन्स बढ़ा लो ।
अमरीका में धाक जमा लो ।।

राजनीतिका चतुर चितेरा, हर पार्टीमें लगा है डेरा ।
हो कोई भी सेनेटर नेता, फोटो सब के संग है मेरा ।
कुर्सी पा और नेता बन, फिर हिमायतियों की ऐसीतेसी ।
भारत की रक्षा के छल से, सबसे अपना काम बना लो ।
अमरीका में धाक जमा लो ।।

- *हिमांशु पाठक*

स्वतन्त्रता !

माँ-बाप की बुद्धि गल गई,
जब पता चला कि
इनकी तेरा साल की लड़की,
गर्भवती हो गई।

बेटी को समझाया,
उसका दर्द बुझाया
गर्भ दवाई से गिर सकता है,
और समाज में होने वाला अपमान,
टल सकता है।

बच्ची बोली - माँ !
पादरी कहते हैं
यह तो है भगवान की देन,
और उसके बिना,
मुझे कैसे होगा चैन !

माँ ने समझाया,
तू अभी बच्ची है,
बच्चा कैसे पालेगी,
पढ़-लिख,
और कुछ बन जा,
नहीं तो जीवन कैसे निकालेगी।

बच्ची ने धमकाया,
अब बात को,
यही तक छोड़िये,
आगे न बढ़ाइये।
अगर बात बढ़ जाएगी,
तो घर से बाहर निकल,
कोर्ट तक जाएगी !

कल ही न्यायालय ने,
अपना पंगु न्याय,
सुनाया है ।
और बच्ची के
होने वाले बच्चे की
परवरिश का जिम्मेदार,
बच्ची के
माँ-बाप को बताया है।

वाह कैसा यह न्याय है ?
कैसी स्वतन्त्रता है ?
कैसा यह प्रजातन्त्र है ?
लोग अपने ही,
बच्चे पालने के लिये,
परतन्त्र हैं !
       परतन्त्र हैं !
              परतन्त्र हैं !

— *हिमांशु पाठक*

खोज

मुझे खोज है उस प्यार की
जिसे रिश्तोंका कोई नाम न हो।
ऐसा भी कोई अपना हो
जिसे खोने का कोई भय भी न हो ।

जहाँ भी देखो रिश्तोंसे बंधा
प्यार बनता सजता है,
हरकोई डरता रहता है,
तभी तो प्यार देता है।
मुझे खोज है उस प्यार की
जिसे डरसे कोई नाता न हो,
ऐसा भी कोई अपना हो
जिसे खोने का कोई भय भी न हो ।

हरेक चहेरे पे देखो सदा
खुशियाँ सजती छलकती रहे।
आज की इस शाम की तरह
रात में दिन ढलता रहे ।
मुझे खोज है उस प्यार की
जिसे ग़मसे कोई नाता न हो ।
ऐसा मेरा एक सपना है
जो प्यारा मेरा अपना है।

- मुझे खोज......।

- जलेन्दु वैद

प्रेमप्रतिज्ञा

कहाँ जा रहे हो, हमें साथ ले लो,
किसी भी राह पर तुम संग चलूंगी ।
न और कुछ भी चाहुँ, न शिकवा करूंगी,
मेरे प्यार का तुम स्वीकार कर लो ।
तुम्हारे लिये ही सजायें हैं सपने
मेरे प्यार की हर तमन्ना है तुम से ।
अगर तुम न अपने संग ले चलोगे
नजरों से बंधे हम पीछे चलेंगे।
मेरे प्यार को हर आशा है तुमसे।
अगर तुम जो अपने संग ले चलोगे,
सहारा बनूंगी, मेरा स्वीकार कर लो ।

– जलेन्दु वैद

Kalpana Singh-Chitnis

22 Creek Road, No. 138, Irvine, CA 92604; She writes Hindi and English poems. She has four collections of poems published, three in Hindi and one in English. She received Rajbhasha Award and Title of Bihar Shree. Her poem has appeared in the poetry collection of The National Library of Poetry, USA. She translates poems and short stories into Hindi, Urdu and English. She has written stories of three screenplays and three films. In addition to M.A. in Political Science, she studied Film Directing at New York Film Academy.

कागज की नाव

मैं अब भी किसी रोज घुप् अंधेरे में
मेज के सामने
कुर्सी पर बैठी
करती हूँ जिंदगी का हिसाब-किताब
मेरी आँखे बंद होती हैं
ओर मेरी उंगलियाँ लिखती हैं....
मेरी उँगलियाँ नहीं रही कभी
रोशनी की मुहताज !
और ऐसे में मन एकाएक
चाहता हैं सब कुछ छोड़ कर
कहीं चल देना !
क्या रखा है जिंदगी के इस हिसान-किताब में ?
नहीं....
मैं नहीं लौटना चाहती

उन शोर भरी गलियों मे फिर !
मैं उठकर देखती हूँ-
स्याह रात में
बरखा की बूंदें गिर रही लगातार
मेरी खिड़कियों के शीशे पर,
और बाहर पानी का रेला ।
और मुझे बस
मन की रिसती दीवारों के
गिरने का इंतजार,
मैं फिर बनाना चाहूँगी
जिंदगी के बाकी बचे सफ़हों से
कागज की एक नाव ।

- कल्पना सिंह चिटनिस

सच

वे कहते हैं
मुझे सच का इल्म नहीं
इसलिए कि जो सच को जानते हैं
वे नहीं होते लापरवाह,
मैं नहीं जानती सच को
इसलिए जब भी किसी ने दस्तक दी
मैंने खोल दिये अपने घर के दरवाजे ।

जो सच को जानते हैं
वे नहीं हँसते बात बे बात ।

मैं नहीं जानती सच को
सो जमाना जानता है आज
मेरे मुंह में कितने दाँत ।

जो सच को जानते है,
वे कुछ भी कहने से पहले
हर बात का वज़न
खूब अच्छी तरह करते हैं
मेरी बातें ढाक के तीन पात,
मेरी बातें जमाने के ठेंगे पर ।

जो सच को जानते हैं-
वे सीखना जरुरी मानते हैं
अपनी दुम हिलाकर
ओर की दुम काबू करना ।
मैंने अपनी दुम गँवा दी
अपने अनाड़ीपन में ।
और अब मेरा हुक्का-पानी
उनके रहमों - करम पर ।

आते,जाते देखते हैं लोग -
मैं गाँव की टेकरी पर बैठी
अश्पृश्य सनकी कुतिया की तरह
पंचों का फैसला होने तक ।

– कल्पना सिंह चिटनिस

दोस्ती का दीप

मैं दोस्ती का दीप
            जलाने आई हूँ...
एक दूजेकों एक दूजेसे
            मिलाने आई हूँ।...

इस गमकी दुनिया में
            है कुछ साथी डूबे डूबे
मिलके आज उन्हें
            मैं मुस्कुराने आई हूँ।...मैं दोस्तीका....

है कुछ जख़्मी
            और दर्दके तूफानमें फँसे
मैं उस जख़्मको
            आज मिटाने आई हूँ ।

मिलना बिछुड़ना यह
            तकदीरका खेल है
जो न मिले उन्हींको
            आज मिलाने आई हूँ।...मैं दोस्तीका.

- कुंदन पटेल

Laxmi Shankar Chowdhury

41, Bunning Dr., Woorheez, NJ 08043; lives in USA for last 35 yrs.; M.S. Eng. from Villanova University; worked over 30 yrs. at various nuclear power plants in Texas, ohio, Michigan, Tennessee, Alabama, New York and New Jersey; started film acting in his daughter's movie; writes Hindi poems and sometime English too; takes active interest in Kavi-Sammelans.

'सुलझन'

सत्य में सुख है,
झूठ एक भुलावा है
स्वप्न में तुम मिले-
सोने के रथ में, अश्व थे फूल के
केशरिया चुनरी में, तन था चम्पा सा
हिरणी सी आँखे और दाँत थे मोती से
दूध की नदियाँ और हीरों के पहाड़ थे
सुषमा थी,
सुरभि थी।
पलक खुली-
जेठ की दोपहरी थी
तवे सी तपती
टामर की सड़कें थी।
सूखे - सूखे पेड़ थे

टूटे - फूटे रिक्शों में
मानव ही अश्व थे।
बदबू थी मीलों की
दर्द था, कोलाहल था ।

तो,

पहले स्वप्न था, मगर सुखद था।

फिर,

जग था, मगर आक्रोश था।

यानि,

जग भूलावा था, उलझन थी ।
स्वप्न मंजुल था, सुलझन थी।

– लक्ष्मी शंकर चौधरी

संगम

मैं तपते सूरज की चकाचौंध,
तुम पूनम चंदा की शीतलता ।

मैं महाभारत का शब्द-कोश,
तुम रामायण की मधु कविता ।

मैं अंधकार के जीवन में डूबु-उभरु,
प्रतिदिन, हर क्षण ।
तुम पीड़ित दुःखमय जीवन को
हर पल आनन्दित करती हो ।

मैं भव्य सागर का खारा पन
तुम पवित्र गंगा की धारा ।

मेरा जीवन है मृग छाया
तेरा जीवन है अनुपम ।

मैं रेगिस्तान का सूखापन,
तुम हो मधुबन की सुंदरता ।

मैं तूफानी दरिया की मझधार,
तुम हो मधुर पायल की झनकार ।

मैं ऊपर चढ़ने में शिथिल
तुम नीचे उतरो तो संगम हो ।

- लक्ष्मी शंकर चौधरी

समझौता

तुम और हम
हो सके तो एक वादा करें ।
कहने की कई बातें हैं ।
कुछ तुम कहो,
कुछ हम कहें ।
वक्त को किसी तरह से बाँट लें ।
फिर कुछ तुम सुनो,
कुछ हम सुनें ।
सीखें सागर के पास से ।
आती – जाती लहरों में
होते होंगे आघात,
मगर प्रत्याघात कभी नहीं ।
चलते हैं संवाद सुनहरे ।
हम भी क्यों न कोशिश करें ?
ऐसा ही एक वादा करें ।
होते हैं मौसम के सुहाने तरीके।
बिख़रती है पतझड़,
निखरती है बहार ।
फिर फूल फूल है बाग बाग,
नयी सी पत्तियाँ सजी हुई।
खुश है हवा के ज़र्रें ज़र्रें ।
हम भी आपस में समझौते करें ।
चलो, एक वादा करें ।

– प्रीति सेनगुप्ता

Dr. Pushplata Sharma

68 Maria Ct., Kendall Park, NJ 08824; she writes poems since many years. She was principal of the Central School at Ahmedabad and possesses M.A. & Ph.D. Her poems have appeared in various magazines & anthologies; her one collection of Hindi poems has been published.

कवि और कविता

कवि चाँद अपनी

कमलिनी कविता से

यूं कुछ पूछने लगा -

कई सदियों से

जब मैं तुझे निहारता हूँ

तब तब तू खिल उठती है

आखिर तेरा मेरा रिश्ता क्या है ?

तू मेरी आत्मा की रागिणी है

मेरी पलकें खुलते ही

तू विहँसने लगती है

किन्तु, आश्चर्य !

मैं हूँ गगन में

तू है धरा पर

मैं हूँ यथार्थ में

हाडमाँस का पुतला

तू है कल्पना के परों पर

मैं और तू
इसी तरह, इस धरा पर
बनते, सँवरते रहते हैं ।
मैं तो नश्वर हूँ
क्योंकि मैं आदमी हूँ
कविते ! प्रिया
तू अनश्वर, शाश्वत है ।
तू अमर रहो ।
विभिन्न रंगों में, पृथ्वी के प्रांगण में
खिल खिलाती रहो
मुझे देखकर ऐसे ही
मुस्कराती रहो
सुगन्ध फैलाती रहो ।

– *पुष्पलता शर्मा*

जगत चक्र

शांत स्थिर पानी में
अचानक एक पत्थर गिरा
लहरें तरंगित हुई
मानों हृदय में एक भूचाल आया
धड़कने तेज़ हुई
सोचा अचानक यह क्या हुआ?
कल तक मैंने देखा था
मेरी खिड़की से
तन्मय हो उन्हें अखबार पढ़ते हुए
प्रश्न उठा - आज कहाँ गए
इस दुनिया से विदा हुए?
क्या अचानक कभी भी
किसी भी क्षण, कोई भी
अपने अखबार की दुनिय।
समेटकर, बटोरकर,
निर्जीव हो इस धरा पर
अपने पार्थिव देह को छोड़कर
पंचभूतो में मिलने के लिए
हमेशा के लिए, चला जाएगा ।
सभी भाई, बेटे, भतीजे
सगे संबंधी क्षण दो क्षण
पार्थिव देह को देखकर

बिलखते हुए द्राह संस्कार,
करने को उतावले हो, निरविलंबित
''राम नाम सत्य हो'' - कहकर
अपना कर्म करते रहो
मानो कंधा देना और जलाना
उनका नित्य कर्म हो
मनुष्य ! इस क्षणभंगुरता
नश्वरता को देखकर भी
तुम अति-प्रसन्न हो
तुम अपनी मोह-माया
पाश में स्वयं जकड़ते
मकड़ी का जाल बनाते हो
जीवन की इस कसक को
तू कहाँ से आया?
क्यों आया? कहाँ जाएगा ?
क्या कभी इसका पता भी पाएगा
इस सृष्टि का चक्र ऐसे ही
चलता है, निरंतर चलता जाएगा ।
जल में पत्थर गिरा है
लहरों की तिरोहित होने दो
जगत् का चक्र यों ही चलता जाएगा
यह नित्य कर्म है, उसे यों ही चलाएगा।

- पुष्पलता शर्मा

Rajni Bhargava

16, Dickinson Ct. Plainsboro, NJ 08536; She writes poerty in Hindi & English since Childhood. Her poems have appeared in Kavyalaya & Anubhuti. She possesses Masters in Sociology from Delhi Univ. and lives in USA for last 18 years.

भ्रम

देखो सखी सूरज ने आज मुझे जगाया ।
ओस की बूँदों ने पैरों को गुदगुदाया ।
गैंदे और गुलाब ने मखमली धूप को सजाया ।
मेरे हाथों की तपिश को गुलाल बना
अपने मुख पर लगाया ।

सुबह की इस आब को,
स्थिर क्षण की इस आस को,
जीवन भर के इस प्रयास को,
नक्षत्र बना आकाश में टांक दिया है
जब टूटेगा, तो अनकही इच्छा बना
फिर इस सुबह को बुला लूँगी
एक और क्षणिक भ्रम बना
सूरज को फिर बुला लूँगी ।

– रजनी भार्गव

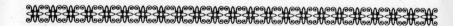

अभिव्यक्तियाँ

सांझ ढलते ढलते मेरे पदचाप ले गई,
मेरी झोली में गुलमोहर व बबूल के फूल दे गई ।
तुम्हारी याद आई तो भीगी पलकों की जगह,
नीले आसमान की गहराई दे गई ।

परिधि के घेरे में आ बैठे हैं,
कुछ चिन्ह नियुक्त कर बैठे हैं ।
उनसे हम जूझ बैठे हैं,
परिधि में अपने आप को खो बैठे हैं ।

इतनी खामोशी से डरते है,
कि खुद भी खामोश हो,
अपने ही पदचापों को सुना करते हैं ।

किताबों में कुछ किस्से हैं,
मेरी उम्र के कुछ गुज़रे हुए हिस्से हैं ।

— रजनी भार्गव

Rakesh Khandelwal

1713 Wilcox Lane, Silver Spring, MD 20906; he writes poetry since school days; his Hindi poetry collection has been published. His poems have appeared in numerous magazines; and have been broadcasted from Radio & TV programs; lives in USA for last 21 years.

चाँदनी की चूनरी

स्वप्न आँखें सजाती रही रात भर, चाँदनी रात की चूनरी के तले,
पर उगी भोर की दस्तकों से सभी, बनके सिन्दूर नभ में बिखरते रहे ।

तारे पलकों पे बैठे रहे रात भर, आने वालों का स्वागत सजाये हुए,
ओस बन कर टपकते रहे राग सब, चाँद के होंठ पर गुनगुनाये हुए,
थाम कर चाँदनी की कलाई हवा, मन के गलियारे में नृत्य करती रही,
कामना एक बन आस्था चल पड़ी आस पी के मिलन की लगाये हुए ।

सात घोड़ों के रथ बैठ आई उषा, एक सन्दूकची थाम कर हाथ में
जिसके दर्पण की परछाइयाँ थाम कर रंग सातों गगन पर सँवरते रहे ।

पग की पाजेब के बोल कुछ बोल कर, थे गुँजाते रहे एक चौपाल को,
रूख कड़े घंटिया के सुरों के मगर, न सफल हो जगा पाये घड़ियाल को,
थरथरा थरथरा दीप तुलसी तले, साँझ से पूर्व ही थक गया सो गया,
रह गया एक पीपल अचंभित खड़ा, होना क्या था मगर क्या से क्या हो गया ।

रोज लाता रहा दिन, कभी साँझ ने, अपने केशों में गजरे लगाये नहीं,
मोतिया, जूही, चंपा, चमेली सभी, रोज कलियों की तरह चटखते रहे ।

- राकेश खंडेलवाल

मंदिरों की घंटियाँ

सुर के तारों से जुड़ न सकी भावना शब्द सब कंठ में छटपटाते रहे.....।
पंथ पर था नजर को बिछाये शिशिर कोई भेजे निमंत्रण उसे प्यार का,
प्रश्न लेकर निगाहें उठीं हर निमिष पर न धागा जुड़ा कोई संचार का,
चाँदनी का बना हमसफ़र हर कोई शेष सब ही को जैसे उपेक्षा मिली,
उठ पुकारें, गगन से मिली थीं गले किन्तु सूनी रही इस नगर की गली ।
टुकड़े टुकड़े बिखरता रहा आस्माँ स्वप्न परवाज़ बिन छटपटाते रहे....।
क्षीण संचय हुआ होम करते हुए गुनगुनाई नहीं आस की बाँसुरी,
मन्त्र ध्वनियाँ धूएं में विलय हो गई भर नहीं पाई संकल्प की आँजुरी,
कोई संदेश पहुँचा नहीं द्वार तक उलझी राहें सभी को निगलती रहीं,
मील का एक पत्थर बनी जिन्दगी उम्र रफ्तार से किन्तु चलती रही ।
प्यास, सावन की अगवानी करती रही मेघ आषाढ़ के घिर के आते रहे....।
भोर उत्तर हुई साँझ दक्षिण ढली पर न पाई कहीं चैन की क्यारियाँ,
स्वप्न के बीज बोये जहाँ थे कभी उग रही हैं वहाँ सिर्फ दुश्वारियाँ,
बिम्ब खोये हैं दर्पण की गहराई में और परछाईं नजरें चुराने लगी,
ताकते हर तरफ कोई दिखता नहीं कैसी आवाज है जो बुलाने लगी ।
कोई सूरत न पहचान में आ सकी रंग भदरंग हो झिलमिलाते रहे .....।
हमने भेजे थे अरमान जिस द्वार पर बंद निकला वही द्वार उम्मीद का,
कोई आकर मिला ही नहीं है गले अजनबी बन के मौसम गया ईद का,
सलवटों में हथेली की खोती रहीं भाग्य ने जो रंगी चन्द राँगोलियाँ,
हमने माणिक समझ कर बटोरा जिन्हें वो थीं टूटी काँच की गोलियाँ ।
राह को भूल वो खो न जाये कहीं सूर्य के पथ में दीपक जलाते रहे....।
है सुनिश्चित कि सूरज उगे पूर्व में आज तक ये बताया गया था हमें,
और ढलना नियति उसकी, पश्चिम में है जिंदगी भर सिखाया गया था हमें,
पर दिशाओं ने षडयंत्र ऐसे रचे भूल कर राह सूरज कहीं खो गया,
एक आवारा बादल भटकता हुआ लाश पर दिन की, दो अश्रु, आ रो गया!
और हम देवताओं की मरजी समझ घंटियाँ मंदिरों की बजाते रहे....।

- राकेश खंडेलवाल

Renu 'Rajvanshi' Gupta

6070 Eaglet Drive, West Chester, OH 45069; writes poetry since many years; she possesses B.A. (Sanskrit) & M.A. (English). She is computer professional and taught Computer Science for many years. She writes short stories too; profession keeps her active in her external life and literature keeps her active in her internal life; published one collection of poems and two collections of short stories.

सागर-बूँद

जो चाहते है सागर उठाना,
सागर की लहरें गिनना,
सागर कों आकाश से मिलाना,
वो करें आकाश-पाताल एक,
अपना अस्तित्व सँवारती,
मैं तो खुश हूँ एक बूँद बनकर ।

बूँद में क्षमता है, सागर का निर्माण करें ।
एक सागर का दूसरे सागर से मिलान करें ।
क्या कभी सागर को, बूँद रचते देखा है?

उसकी पीड़ा बाँटने के लिए, बूँद बनते देखा है?
बूँद-बूँद ही से तो सागर बनते हैं ।
क्या कभी सागर गागर में सिमटते हैं?
सृष्टि के निर्माण की सहभागी,

मैं खुश हूँ एक बूँद बनकर ।

बूँद को अपने अस्तित्व का भान है ।

जीवन है भंगुर, इसकी पहचान है ।

रचने की क्षमता है, वो कर्मरत दिन-रात है ।

सागर को है अपने आकार पर अभिमान ।

नहीं घटा है युगों-युगों से, बन गया है जड़-आलस्य-प्रमाद ।

पीड़ा नहीं झेली रचने की इसने, फिर किस कर्म पर है इसे अभिमान ।

जीने के लिए क्षण - क्षण चेतती,

मैं तो खुश हूँ एक बूँद बनकर ।

समय की झोली में अर्पण कर, आगे बढ़ जाऊँगी अनंत पथ पार ।

समा जाएगा मुझमें, यह सागर अनंत अपार ।

धरा के कोने - कोने पर, होगा मेरा विस्तार ।

परंतु क्या नाम था मेरा, यह भी ना जान पाएगा संसार ।

अंत को अनंत से मिलाती,

खुश हूँ मैं एक बूँद बनकर ।

- रेणु 'राजवंशी' गुप्ता

ये बच्चे हैं मेहमान घर के

ये बच्चे हैं मेहमान घर के,
आज आए हैं कल चले जाएँगे ।
जाकर फिर लौट आएँगे,
और मिलकर चले जाएँगे ।

तुम करना इनका स्वागत - सत्कार,
परंतु करना नहीं व्याकुल हो इंतजार ।
ये आते रहें अपनी इच्छा से,
ना हो कोई बंधन ना हो गुहार ।
तुम खुले रखना अपने घर के द्वार ।
ये बच्चे हैं मेहमान घर के ।

रखना इनका कमरा साज-सँवार,
होता है सुखद अपने पलंग पर सोना पाँव पसार ।
बनाना इनकी पसंद के माल-पकवान,
खिलाना मन से, पर करना नहीं अधिक मान-मनुहार ।
ये बच्चे हैं मेहमान घर के ।

जब आएँ बच्चे घर अपने,
हो तुम्हारे नेहरे पर ताजी मुसकान ।
तुम दिखो इन्हें स्वस्थ, तुम रहना सदैव प्रसन्न,
करना नहीं इनसे अपनी समस्या का बखान,
ये बच्चे हैं मेहमान घर के ।

रखना नहीं कोई काम इनके लिए,
ये आते है घर आराम के लिए ।
तुम ग्रोसरी स्वयं लाना, कार में गैस स्वयं भरवाना,
रखना नहीं इनके कंधों पर अपना भार ।
ये बच्चे हैं मेहमान घर के ।

- रेणु 'राजवंशी' गुप्ता

Sarojini Sharma

90, Nathaniel Street, Torrington, CT 06790; she writes poems in Hindi & English since childhood. Her poems & articles published in different Anthologies, magazines & newspapers; recipient of Editor's Choice Award from National Library of Poetry (1997) and International Poet of Merit Award from the International Society of Poets (2003); M.A., B.T. from Agra University; worked as lecturer at Govt. Girls' H.S. School, Delhi for many years; lives in USA for the last 32 years.

काव्य का सृजन

यदि जीवन की व्यथा हृदय को विचलित नहीं करती,
तो मानव में भावनाओं की उत्पत्ति नहीं होती,
यदि उर में कुछ भाव न उगते,
तो जीवन नीरस ही होता ।
भावुकता ही है काव्य की जननी,
संवेदना है भाव हृदय के,
यदि मानव उर पाषाण बन गया,
तो है निधन काव्य-सृजन का ।
अन्तरतम की व्यथा मनुज को,
मानवता ही सिखलाती है,
जीवन में कुछ प्रगति करने की,
क्षमता ही उसमें तब आती है ।
तुलसीदास वाल्मीकि आदि कवि,
जो कि साधारण से पुरुष थे,
अन्तरतम उर व्यथा से व्यथित हो,
रामायण महान काव्य रच डाले ।
उर व्यथा ही है काव्य की जननी,
भावुकता ही है कवि की लेखनी,
दोनों ही के सम्मिश्रण से,
हो जाता है काव्य का सृजन ।

– सरोजिनी शर्मा

उर की सुन्दरता

उर की सुन्दरता के समक्ष,

    तन की सुन्दरता कुछ भी नहीं,
मानव का उर यदि सुन्दर हो,

    तो इसकी जरूरत कुछ भी नहीं,
तन की सुन्दरता क्षणिक सदा,

    जो आयु के साथ बदलती है,
उर की सुन्दरता सदैव अमर,

    जो सदैव ही अमर रहती है ।
यौवन की अन्धी मादकता में,

    जब मानव मदहोश हो जाता है,
तो जीवन की थोथी मादकता में,

    बेबस हो बह जाता है ।
जब होश आता है रोता है,

    जीवन की इस सच्चाई को,
तब समझ कहीं वह पाता है,

    उर की सुन्दरता के समक्ष,
वह नतमस्तक हो जाता है ।

    मानवता है तन की सुन्दरता,
सुन्दरता है कुछ और नहीं,

    उर की सुन्दरता के समक्ष,
तन की सुन्दरता कुछ भी नहीं ।

– सरोजिनी शर्मा

Dr. Sudarshan 'Priyadarshini'

647, Tollis Pky, Broadview Heights, OH, 44147. She writes poetry not as passion, but as a form of self-therapy. In addition to poetry, she writes novels & Short stories. Her published books include one collection of poems, three novels and one collection of short stories. Her poems have appeared in several Anthologies. She received Mahadevi Award from Hindi Parishad, Toronto; Governor's Media Award, Ohio and Award of Appreciation from the Federation of India N.E. Ohio. She is Ph.D.(Hindi) from Punjab Univ. and lives in USA for the last 22 years. She was the editor of a cultural magazine "Fragrance" and produced a Radio-Show & a TV-Show for the Indo-American audiance. She taught a course "Non-Western Culture : India" at the Cleveland State University.

सारभौम

अपनी ही
सांसों के बवंडर
में डूब-उतर
रही हूँ ।

आस-पास
दूर - दूर तक
लहरों की
मायावी - तरंगे
अलोप हो गई है ।

क्षितिज का कहीं -
कोई किनारा
सुरमयी - सौरभ
और सतरंगी
ऊहापोह में
डूबा होगा शायद ।

मेरे आसपास
तो बस -
संध्या की कोयल
की कूक
भी मध्यम पड़
गई है.......

और उम्र का
सूनापन -
अपने पूरे
सारभौम
में उतर आया है ।

– *सुदर्शन'प्रियदर्शिनी'*

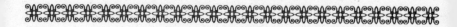

शुभ कामना

इतनी दूर
नहीं पहुँचेगी
तुम्हें मेरी शुभ कामनाएँ
समय रहते।
क्यों कि, न जाने
कितने देशों की
खाक छान कर पहुँचेगा
मेरा तुम तक
यह कार्ड।
तब तक-
उस पर लग चुका होगा
अनंत देशों की
आपसी फुटौवल
हिंसा - ईर्ष्या और
मन - मुटौवल का
गहरा दाग .... ।
तब तक नव वर्ष की -
इन शुभकामनाओं
और स्नेह से भीगी
भावनाओं की ठण्डी
पड़ चुकी होगी -
यह आग ..... ।

- सुदर्शन 'प्रियदर्शिनी'

Surendranath Tiwari

23, County Road 519, Newton, NJ 07860; he writes Hindi Poems since many years; drawing inspiration from the village-life of India and Gandhian philosophy. He was the president of the International Hindi Samiti and keeps deep interest in the Indian Culture & Heritage. He lives in USA for the last 25 years; his one book of Hindi poems published in 2001. He has graduated with Civil Eng. and has M.E. (Eng. Management) & M.B.A. from Ohio State University; he was commissioned officer in Indian Army; he was teaching Eng. Management at the Universities in Ohio & New Jersey. He was member of the Advisory Committee of the Civil Eng. Dept. of The Ohio State Univ. He is associated with the Energy Projects of USA.

स्वागत है नई सदी का

तम के तारों को समेट कर
अवगाहित कर उन्हें उदधि में
यह जो उतर रही है ऊषा,
प्राची क्षितिज के स्वर्णांचल पर।
मानव के अज्ञान तमस को तज,
निशीथ को वर्ण - भेद कर,
यह जो अरुण रूप निखरा है,
भाव - भास्वर का उदयाचल पर।

भारत की अस्मिता अखंडता
भारतीयों का मूल - मंत्र हो।
एक व्यक्ति की नहीं, देश की
उन्नति हेतु सभी तंत्र हों।
प्रजातंत्र के लेबल केवल
दरवाजों पर नहीं लगे हों।

सब आयामों में समाज के
सच्चा, जीवित, प्रजातंत्र हो ।
जाति - भेद से परे हो भारत
अपना देश सभी का ।
स्वागत है नई सदी का ।

इनमें छिपी हुई हैं किरणें
मानवता के नव-भविष्य की,
इन किरणों से ज्योतित होगा
उन्नत भाल मही का ।
स्वागत है नई सदी का ।

गंगा - वोल्गा- हडसन मिल
हर मन के मैल मिटाएं ।
क्षितिज बनेगी यह जगती,
टूटेंगी सब सीमाएं ।
मनुजत्व पुन: जागेगा,
वसुधा को कुटुंब बनाकर,
मानव का गौरव होंगी,
वेदों की महिम ऋचाएं ।
नरता का उदयाचल होगा,
भारत यह नई सदी का ।
स्वागत है नई सदी का ।

इंटरनेट जैसे यंत्रों से
दुनिया एक गांव बनेगी ।
देशों की ही नहीं, दूरी
जन-मन की भी कम होगी ।
नव-सौहार्द का क्षितिज खुलेगा
नये मनुज की अगवानी में ।
मानवत्व- गौरव हेतु यह
सदी अन्यतम होगी ।

मंगल - ग्रह पर मानव - गृह की
नींव पड़ेगी इसी सदी में,
स्वर्ण काल होगा नरता का,
प्रकृति - नटी का टीका ।
स्वागत है नई सदी का ।

एक प्रश्न पर साल रहा :
क्या पुन: सभ्यता नंगी होगी?
या मर्यादा के आंचल में छिपी रहेगी मानव-लज्जा ?
महुए-चंदन से महकेंगे, घर - आँगन, बगिया, सरेह या,
फैक्ट्रियों की धूम-धमक से होगी इस धरती की सज्जा ?
क्या उन्नति की भाग दौड़ में कुचली जाएगी मानवता ?
हम परिवार जिसे कहते, क्या रह जाएगी उसकी सत्ता ?
नव-शिशु के क्रंदन की खुशियां, मिलन-विरह की व्याकुलताएं,
मानव-मन की मृदुल तंत्रियाँ- प्रणय-प्रेम की परिभाषाएं ।
यंत्रों के कर्कश निनाद में वीणा के स्वर खो जाएंगे ?
डूबेगा क्या दिल का सरगम, भूलेंगी मन की भाषाएं ?
प्रश्नों, आशाओं का संगम, मनुज-सभ्यता का चौराहा ।
संदेहों, आकांक्षाओं से, भरे हुए ये अद्भुत हैं क्षण ।
ये पहली किरणें शताब्दि की, जाने क्या लेकर आई हैं:
नर-प्रज्ञा के नये शिखर, या नरता-घाती हिंसक बम ?
लेकिन विश्वासों के बल पर
मानवता विकसित होती है ।
आओ संदेहों को तज,
मानवता में विश्वास करें हम ।
शुभम् - स्वप्न से शुरू करें यह
स्वर्ण-शतक जगती का।
स्वागत है नई सदी का ।
स्वागत है नई सदी का

- सुरेंद्रनाथ तिवारी

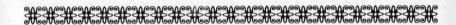

तड़पते मनुष्य से

सुन विकल, विह्वल मनुज रे,
आज युग क्या चाहता है ?

युद्ध के भीषण झकोरे
पाप की विकराल ज्वाला ?
या अमित संतप्त मानव के
रगों की लाल हाला ?

हाँ! मनुज का तो नहीं, पर मनुजता का खून !

भूख की चिल्लाहटों में
आदमीपन खो गया है ।
जो हुआ अब तक नहीं था,
आज वह सब हो गया है ।

कोकिला के कंठ-स्वर से
नाश की धुन आ रही है ।
जो रही अब तक मनुज में
वह मनुजता जा रही है ।

अंततः यह बात क्यों है?
यह नवल आघात क्यों है ?
मूल क्या है इस प्रलय का?
पाप के नाशक निलय का?

मूल पाना चाहते हो?
तोड़ दो दीवार मन की ।
और देखो जल रही है
ये कहाँ लपटें अनल की ।

पाप की यह वह्नि तुझको
है मिली मनुजत्व खोकर,
इसलिए तुम मिट रहे हो
इस तरह संतप्त होकर ।

सुन रहे हो यह प्रलय का
शोर, जो तुम आज जग में,
वह मिला है रे मनुज को
मनुजता से हीन मग में ।

खो दिया तुमने मनुज जो
वह सृजन का मूल था रे !
आदमीपन इस चमन के,
पत्थरों में फूल था रे !

उस सृजन के मूल हेतु
मनुज, मिटना ही पड़ेगा
एक रूठे फूल हेतु
मनुज, मिटना ही पड़ेगा ।

आज रूठी मनुजता को
तो मनाना ही पड़ेगा ।
त्याग की उस वेदी तक तो
मनुज, जाना ही पड़ेगा ।

आज अपनापन मिटाकर,
स्वत्व का बलिदान देकर,
हृदय के मधुकुंड की
पावन हवि में प्राण देकर ।

दूसरों के हित जिओ तुम
दूसरों के हित मरो रे ।
मनुज ! फिर से मनुजता हित
त्याग का संचय करो रे !

– सुरेंद्रनाथ तिवारी

Ved Prakash "Vatuk"

P.O.Box 1142, Berkeley, CA 94701; he writes in Hindi & English: poetry, essays, memoirs etc., he is the writer & editor of many books related to Linguistics, Folk-literature & Humanism; he is the author of over 20 published books including collection of Hindi poems, he was teaching Linguistics, Folk-literature & Cultural Heritage of India for about 30 years at the universities in the states of Colorado, California & Illinois; he worked as the editor of several magazines; he is associated with various literary, cultural & social organizations; he carried out his higher education at the universities of Agra (India), London and also at the Harvard University, USA; he received D.Lit.Degree on the basis of the comparative study of Sanskrit & old Church Slavonik language; he was the secretary of the Hindi Parishad-London during the period when he was in U.K.; his writings have been broadcasted on B.B.C.; he did research on the life of the Indian Immigrants; at present he is the Director of Folk-Lore Institute at Berkeley, California; he has been honoured by various national & International literary & social organizations and the Hindi Academy of Uttar-Pradesh honoured him with "First Non-resident Indian Hindi Bhushan" Award; he lives in USA for the last 35 years.

मैं नहीं मानता

जो ढहाता है नित प्यार का हर किला,
जिससे आपस में कोई नहीं हो मिला,
हो कुरुक्षेत्र में या जुटें करबला,
भाई-भाई का ही काटे जिससे गला,
ऐसे हर धर्म को, पाप-दुष्कर्म को,

मैं नहीं मानता, मैं नहीं मानता ।
बेकसों का जलाता है जो आशियाँ,
चमन को ही उजाड़े जहाँ बागबाँ,
जो भरे दिन को भी कर दे काली अमा,
जहर ही के धुएँ से भरे आसमाँ,
ऐसे उपदेश को, दानवी भेष को,
मैं नहीं मानता, मैं नहीं मानता ।

शर्म जिनको जरा भी है आनी नहीं,
है रुधिर आँख में, करुणा जानी नहीं,
प्यास बुझने को दो बूँद पानी नहीं,
खूनी नदियाँ बहाने में सानी नहीं,
ऐसे रहबर का मन, साधुओं का वचन,
मैं नहीं मानता, मैं नहीं मानता ।

बेड़ियाँ हर कदम पर जकड़ती रहें,
नित गुलामी की परतें सौ बढ़ती रहें,
जिससे परदेश की गलियाँ भरती रहें,
कमसिनें गाँव की कलियाँ सड़ती रहें,
ऐसे व्यापार को, काले बाजार को,
मैं नहीं मानता, मैं नहीं मानता ।

चाहे त्रेता में हो, चाहे द्वापर में हो,
हो आयोध्या में या हस्तिनापुर में हो,
जिसमें सीताएँ होती रहेंगी दफन,
द्रौपदी का उतरता रहेगा वसन,
जिसमें शम्बूक सब कत्ल होते रहें,
उँगलियाँ जिसमें एकलव्य खोते रहें,

उस धरम-राज को, ऋषि-मुनी-काज को,
मैं नहीं मानता, मैं नहीं मानता ।
दाने-दाने को मोहताज़ बहुजन रहे,
एक ही वर्ग का नित्य शासन रहे,
अपनी भाषा भिखारिन हो, मोहताज़ हो,
घोर अंग्रेज़ियत का जहाँ राज हो,
उस प्रजातंत्र को, घोर षड्यंत्र को,
मैं नहीं मानता, मैं नहीं मानता ।

अपना घर तो है उनसे संभलता नहीं,
अपने भूखों का है पेट पलता नहीं,
बस इसी आस में साँस जिनके चलें,
गैर का घर जले, हाथ वे सेंक ले,
उन लुटेरो का मन, उनके झूठे वचन,
मैं नहीं मानता, मैं नहीं मानता ।

एक भी व्यक्ति की लाश पर हो खड़ा,
एक भी व्यक्ति का रक्त जिस पर चढ़ा,
हो किसी देश के पुण्यतम धाम में,
हो खुदा का या हो राम के नाम में,
भव्यतम हो विरल, उसको पूजा का थल,
मैं नहीं मानता, मैं नहीं मानता ।

है शहीदों की हमको कसम दोस्तों,
फिर निभानी है उनकी रसम दोस्तों,
उनके पथ से ज़रा भी हटाता है जो,
एक जन का सपन भी मिटाता है जो,
ऐसे मजमून को, काले कानून को,
मैं नहीं मानता, मैं नहीं मानता ।

- वेद प्रकाश 'वटुक'

हर धर्म युद्ध में

हर धर्मयुद्ध में
विजय राम की होती है,
पर मुक्ति रावण को मिलती है ।
और राज्य प्राप्त होता है विभीषणों को
रही सत्य की सीता
उसे मिलेंगे
अग्नि-परीक्षा
वनवास
और
धरती में समा जाना ।

- वेद प्रकाश 'वटुक'

सात सात बहनों के बीच कविता बड़ी हुई

सात सात बहनों के बीच कविता बड़ी हुई ।
प्रीति, बुद्धि, लक्ष्मी, विद्या, कीर्ति, दुनियादारी, जिम्मेदारी,
और सब से छोटी वह खुद - कविता ।
विद्या के प्रति उसे लगन थी,
प्रीति उसके दिल में बस गई थी,
और उसका हाथ थामे वह वनोपवन में टहलनेको चल पड़ती थी;
किन्तु दूसरी ऐसी तेजस्वी बहनों की ओर से भी
उसे असंतोष मिला -
प्रलोभन का भार रहा, आदेश का दबाव सहा,
और उपदेश भी पुरजोश मिला ।
दुनिया में उसका नाम पुकार पुकारकर बुलानेवाले लोग बहुत मिलें,
किन्तु उसके हृदय के कंप, कंप की गति समझनेवाले साहिर कम मिले ।
बहुत सुकुमार वय में वह एकांत में जाकर खड़ी हुई,
सात सात बहनों के बीच कविता बड़ी हुई ।
दुनियादारी ने उसे बहुत समझाया,
कीर्ति ने कौशल से उसे बहुत मनाया,
जिम्मेदारी ने गंभीरता से ज्ञान बाँटा ;
किन्तु कमरे में लौटते ही उसने तो भगवान के पास
गीत का ही वरदान माँगा ।
आखिर लक्ष्मी ने क्रोध में आकर बोलना तक छोड़ दिया,
और बुद्धि ने बीच में टपक-टपककर अवरोध किया,
कीर्ति ने सविनय रिश्ता तोड़ दिया;
पर ऐसी सब तकरारें तो कब नहीं संसार में इस छिड़ी हुई !
सात सात बहनों के बीच कविता बड़ी हुई ।

- विराफ कापडिया

मकान और वृद्ध

खड़े खड़े सोचता है मकान यह
जवान कोई आ जाये मालिक यहाँ
तो हो सकती है मेरी कुछ मरम्मत
जिसकी की मुझको है जरुरत ।

और उस वृद्ध को भी
आते है खयाल बहुत खिडकी पर खड़े खड़े -
निकलूं मैं, निकल चलूं कब यहां से,
न अपना कोई मकान हो,
न मकान के कई काम हो,
सभी काम तमाम हो,
विक्रय में थोड़े- बहुत दाम मिले,
आराम ही आराम हो ।

सोचता है मकान यह पृथ्वी पर जड़ा जड़ा -
मेरी इस समता में, वृद्धि की ममता में,
मेरी ही क्षय है, मेरा ही विलय है ।
सोचता है वृद्ध वह खिड़की पर खड़ा खड़ा -
मकान को बेच - बाच किराये पर रहने में
कितने सब जोख़िम है, कितने ही भय है ।

- विराफ कापडिया

INDO-AMERICAN LITERARY ACADEMY'S

ANTHOLOGY OF POEMS (2005)

ગુજરાતી વિભાગ

Adil Mansuri

P.O.Box 922, Hoboken, NJ 07030; lives in USA for last 20 Yrs.; Writes since young age in Gujarati, Urdu and Hindi; Eminent poet having received kaka kalelkar, kavi kalapi and Chunilal Mehta Awards; honored by the Mayor of Jersey City for his outstanding Literary Contribution. He is Incharge of "SANTH DIN" Group of Gujarati poets meeting almost alternate month; published 9 poetry collections and edited 3 poetry collections; editor of GHAZAL GURJARI. COM Website-magazine for Ghazal poems.

પહેલી જ રાત છે.

ઝુલ્ફોના અંધકારની પહેલી જ રાત છે,
ને સ્પર્શ આરપારની પહેલી જ રાત છે.
કોમળ કળીની આંખમાં ખુશ્બૂ છલક છલક,
આ બાગમાં બહારની પહેલી જ રાત છે.
આ ગુલબદન તો ફૂલની કળી લચક લચક,
કે મુગ્ધતાના ભારની પહેલી જ રાત છે.
અભિસારિકાની ચાલ થનન થન બહક બહક,
સૌંદર્યના ખુમારની પહેલી જ રાત છે.
તારા વદનના રંગના રેલા ફલક ફલક,
શું પૂર્ણિમાના પ્યારની પહેલી જ રાત છે?
મેંદીભરેલ હાથનાં સપનાં પલક પલક,
રંગીન ઇંતેઝારની પહેલી જ રાત છે.
પાલવ ભરેલ તારલા મનમાં મલક મલક,
ઘૂંઘટમઢી સવારની પહેલી રાત જ છે.
સ્નેહીજનો કબરમાં ઉતારી જતાં રહ્યાં,
આદિલ જુદા પ્રકારની પહેલી જ રાત છે.

- આદિલ મન્સુરી

કોને ખબર

બરફના ડુંગરા ખડકતો,
આ ઝંઝાવાત ક્યારે અટકશે ?
કોને ખબર ?
મેનહટ્ટન ગાર્મેન્ટ ડિસ્ટ્રિક્ટની
સાઇડવૉક પર આખ્ખી દુનિયાનાં
કપડાં સીવતાં સીવતાં
કાળમીંઢ સમયના હાથે
પથ્થર થઇ ગયેલો દરજી
તેની કટાઇ ગયેલી સોયથી
પહેરણ સીવી આપે
તેની રાહ જોતો
આ ઉઘાડદેહી હબસી
પોતાના ઘેર પહોંચવાનો
રસ્તો જ ભૂલી ગયો છે.

— આદિલ મન્સુરી

Dr. Arun Mehta

19, Highland Drive, Parlin, NJ 08859; Medical Practitioner (MBBS) having keen interest in Gujarati literature, Writes Ghazals and devotional songs; read his poems in many kavi sammelans; Editor of "Lad Pratibimb" - trimonthly magazine of Lad Samaj of USA; achieved "Person of the Year" award (2004) by Lad Samaj of North America; active member of the Gujarat Medical Association.

ભાવોનું દર્પણ

પ્રત્યેક અજબ શી ચીજમાં અઢળક જમા આ ચહેરો,
રાખે ના કાંઇ છૂપું, છો ને પડદામાં આ ચહેરો;

રંગીન ખૂબ ખૂબ ને વિચિત્ર છે આ ચહેરો,
બદલાય રંગો પળ પળ તે ભાવમાં આ ચહેરો;

રજૂઆત આગવી આ હંમેશ કરતો ચહેરો,
ગૂઢ વાત તુર્ત કહી દે પળવારમાં આ ચહેરો;

કહેવાનું હોય જે કંઇ આલેખ્યું છે લલાટે,
દર્દો હૃદયના કહી દે છે મૌનમાં આ ચહેરો;

સાક્ષી છે સર્વ ઋતુઓનો આ ગજબનો ચહેરો,
છૂપ્યો વસંત પાનખરના ભેદમાં આ ચહેરો;

ગયા અણગમાનો કરતો એકરાર સ્પષ્ટ આ ચહેરો,
પડઘાર્યે નયનના બદલાતા રંગોમાં આ ચહેરો;

અણજાણ કોઇ છે ના, જોતાં કળાય આ ચહેરો,
ભાવોનું છે આ દર્પણ, કહી દે પળમાં આ ચહેરો.

– અરુણ મહેતા

Dr. Bhagirath Majmudar

3220, Olde Dekalb Way, Atlanta, GA 30340 : writes poems & articles; Medical Practioner in Pathology (M.D.); professor of Pathology at Amory University, Atlanta; also associated with Henry Grady Hospital; Gold Medalist in Sanskrit; writes Gujarati poems; his poems published in several magazines.

સુવર્ણ - સંકલ્પો

રહું સહું આ રતીભાર સોનું
ને ઘાટ મારે ઘડવા હજારો.

જ્યાં આવડ્યા ઘાટ હજાર ત્યારે,
રહું સહું આ રતીભાર સોનું.

છોને રહું આ રતીભાર સોનું
ના ઘાટ શાને ઘડવા હજારો?

ઘડી રહ્યો ઘાટ હજાર ચિત્તમાં,
ના ઘાટ બેઠો કદી એક ઘાટનો.

દોડી રહી આ ઘટમાળ ઘાટની
તાકી રહેતાં રતીભાર સોનું.

ઉડી ગયું આ અણમોલ ફોતરું
હજાર ઘાટો નદી ઘાટ ગોઠવી.

- ભગીરથ મજમુદાર

Dr. Bharat Thakkar

1801 Schillerstrom Ct. Wheaton, Illinois 60187; writes mostly poetry for the last 45 years in Gujarati & English. He has published over 9 books; Recipient of Gold Medal from Gujarati Literary Conference, Award from Gujarat State Govt. (1968). His poems appeared in various Anthologies. His English poem was judged by the National Library of Poetry, USA as a top ranking one; living in USA for the last 40 years, possesses M.S. & Ph.D. in Mech. Eng. from Illinois Inst. of Tech.; Sr. Engineer at Lucent Technologies; Part-time professor at Ill. Inst. of Tech.; formerly Chairman of Mech. Eng. Dept. at Midwest college of Eng., Lombard, Ill.

હવે થવું શાંત મારે

હવે થવું શાંત મારે
વિષાદની પળોમાં શમી નવું અકાળે !
અનન્ય અનોખી અનેરીની શોધમાં
વિહ્વળ ના થવું મારે
અનાગતા અલૌકિક અજાણી આકૃતિમાં
ખોવાઇ ના જવું લગારે
હવે થવું શાંત મારે.

એના સ્વરૂપને પામવા મથું વારે વારે
એના નમણાં નયન
સુરમ્ય નમણી નાસિકા
અધરોની લાલિમા, લાલિત્યમાં ડૂબી જવું એ વિચારે
હવે થવું શાંત મારે.

ઊકળાટ, અકળાટ, અજંપો, અધીરાઇ ફરી વળે
કીડીયારુંની જેમ ચૌંટી વળે શરીરે..
ચટકા તીણા ભરે, ક્ષીણા, તીખા–ગમે, ના ગમે;
પરખાય ના એનું મુખારવિંદ
ઓળખાય ના એનો આતમા
ગંભીર, ભેદી, અજાણીને જાણવા મથું આખરે
અનાગતાનો સ્પર્શ છલકાય અંતરે ભલે
પામ્યા છતાં અપ્રાપ્તિના ક્ષોભમાં કે શોકમાં
જીવનનાં અંતકાળે
હવે થવું શાંત મારે !

– ભરત ઠક્કર

સજીવતા

અહીં કબરના પગ આગળ
ફૂલ ખીલેલા જોઉં છું.
ત્યારે આખાય દૃશ્યમાં
પેલા મૃત જીવની સજીવતા અનુભવાય છે.
એ ફૂલોના રંગોમાં
પેલા મૃતનું હૃદય પરખાય છે.
એ મૃતને
મૃત્યુ દરિયા તળેથી મોટી કંદરા ખોદી
કબર તળે આવી
શિયાળવાંની જેમ ઉપાડી જાય.
મૃત્યુ એના શયનખંડમાં
દીવાલો પર કેટલાંક મૃતને ટાંગી દિયે.
એ એના પ્રદર્શનનો ઓરડો
ક્યારેક એની હિંમત ને શોખ માટે
એને પ્રેરણા અર્પે.
કબરો આગળ ખીલેલાં ફૂલ તોડી લાવી
મૃત્યુ દરેક મૃતને શણગારે.
એનો ય જીવ માનવી જેવો !
સજીવતા એને ય ગમતી હોય છે !

– ભરત ઠક્કર

Chandrakant P. Desai

I, Lindsey Ct. Franklin Park, NJ 08823, ph: (732) 821-1272 writing poems for last 50 years; some nonfiction too, in Gujarati & English; published 11 books, 7 of which are poetry collections in Gujarati; Founder & Convener of Indo-American Literary Academy meeting at Barnes & Noble; Mayor of Franklin Twp Ms. Shirley Eberly honoured him at Munic. Council meeting for his contribution in English poetry; New Jersey Poetry Society awarded him II prize in poetry Competition and honourably mentioned thrice for his poems; Premanand Sahitya Sabha awarded his poem I - prize in the Poetry Competition in 1960s. He is the first Indo-American poet invited to read his patriotic poem at the Congressman's inauguration at Capitol Hill, Wash., D.C. He was consulting Engineer for 17 years in various American Engineering firms & lives in USA for the last 29 years. He did postgraduate Eng. Research in Rogowski Institute, Tech. University, Aachen, Germany (1958-60); he was Professor of Elec. Eng. at M.S. Univ. of Baroda & at S.V. Regional Engineering college, Surat for 20 years; Senate & Syndicate member of the South Gujarat University for several years, Dean of the Engineering Faculty of S.G. University in 1976; Ex-president of the Federation of all India Regional Engg. College Teachers' Associations, Ex-president of the S.V. Regional Engg. College Teachers' Association & non-teaching staff Association, Surat, India. Director of the German Language Course at S.G. University, Surat for 7 years; knows Gujarati, Hindi, English, German, Spanish. New Jersey's popular Daily "STAR LEDGER" interviewed him & published it praising him for his outstanding efforts in promoting Indian cultural heritage and awakening consciousness of Indo-Americans to distinguish themselves in American literary world; elected thrice as somerset County Committee Member in general elections (2000-06); Member of the Human Relations Commission of Franklin Twp. In 1960s, he was invited by All India Radio Station, Baroda for Poetry Readings. Collection of poems of famous German poet Reiner Maria Rilke translated directly from German into Gujarati by him will be published shortly, by Gangotri Trust founded by Top ranking poet Mr. Umashankar Joshi.

ઇન્ડોઅમેરિકી રમણી

ન્યૂયોર્કી સબવેમાં ભાળી અલ્લડ એક
       ઇન્ડોઅમેરિકી રમણી;
હડસન સમ અક્કડ ને ફક્કડ પણ જમનાના
       નીર સમી શ્યામળ ને નમણી.
પ્હાનીથી વેંત ઊંચા ડેનિમ બ્લ્યૂ જીન્સ તણી
       છટા એની જબરી જલીમ,
આભ જાણે આવ્યું નીચે ઉતરી ને છાઇ ગઇ
       બીજ તણી શોભા બંકિમ;
ઉમટી પડી હૈયામાં ધડકન અણધારી કૈંક
       સામટીક બમણી ને તમણી.
બિંદિયા માથે ને લિપ્સ ભીનાં ઓરેન્જ, લીલી
       રીસ્ટ વોચ ચમકંતી કાંડે,
કોલર છે વ્હાઇટ, રેડ જેકેટ, બ્લ્યૂ જીન્સ, જાણે
       ફ્લેગ રૂડા સબવેમાં ઊડે;
ભારતીય અમેરિકી ત્રિરંગી રંગોની
       રેશમિયા ભવ્ય શી મેળવણી !
એક આંખ પૂરવની પ્રીતે પલળીને ભીની
       લજ્જાના ઝૂલણિયે ઝૂલે,
બીજી તે પશ્ચિમના વાયરે વિંધાઇ, રૂડા
       રોક એન્ડ રોલ નૃત્યમાં પ્રફુલ્લે;
ધરતીના કંપ બધા ભરીને ઉલ્લાળે એ તો
       ઊંચી એડી ડાબી ને જમણી.
ઘડીભર નીરખીને મને કેમ છો, કાકા? કહીને
       મધમીઠું મલકી એ તો એવું !
સાંભળ્યું તે સાચકલું, તોય મને લાગતું એ
       અપ્સરાના ગીત સૂણ્યા જેવું;
કેશ ભલે શ્વેત, મારી છલકે હૈયાંની હેલ
       નાર દીઠી જાણે પદમણી.

              – ચંદ્રકાંત દેસાઈ

કવિતાની આત્મકથા

(મિશ્રોપજાતિ)

નિ:શબ્દતાની હું રસાર્દ્ર સ્ફૂર્તિ,
અગાધ આશ્લેષતી મુગ્ધ મૂર્તિ;
અમૂર્ત તોયે કવિની કરાંગુલી
મને ચાહે શબ્દ મહીં સુગૂંથવા.

(વસંતતિલકા)

સીતા તણી ગહન શોકની વાટિકાઓ
વીંધી, સહ્યો પ્રખર દ્રૌપદીરોષ અગ્નિ;
ને મેઘદૂતપ્રણયોન્મત્ત શોકપંથે
મ્હાલી, કર્યા નવલ નિત્ય પ્રવાસ મોટા,
ડાબા કરે યુગયુગોય ઘણા રમાડ્યા.

(મિશ્રોપજાતિ)

ના વ્યાસની લેખિનીથી વહીને
ધરાઇ હું, વાલ્મિકી કાલિદાસ
શેકસપિયર હોમરહસ્ત ચૂમી
લોભાઇ ના યોગિની પ્રાજ્ઞ બુદ્ધા;
કૈં કેટલાની ઉરદેવડી થઇ,
તોયે હજી અન્ય અનેક હૈયાં
ચોર્યે જવાં એ જ મને અભીપ્સા.
છંદે મને પૂરી છળે કવિજનો,
છતાં હું સહેજે ન છળાઇ કો'થી;

અનંત વૈવિધ્યની હું પૂજારિણી,
સ્વચ્છંદી આનંદમયી મનીષીની;
સૌ છંદ લાલિત્ય લયો તણા બંધ
તોડી વીંધી વહે નિત મોકળાશે,
આ વિશ્વને ઘેલું કરંત મુજમાં.

(વસંતતિલકા)

ના થાકી હું, હજીય જવું સુદૂર ઊંચી
ટોચે તીણી મનુજ જ્યાં ન દબાય દૈન્યે;
ને ગર્વગર્ત મહીં જાય પડી ન, એને
અનૃત ન ભક્ષ કરી જાય તમિસ્રદંતે;
જ્યાં માનવીહૃદયવારિધિને કિનારા
ના હોય, ને શીતળ ચેતનચંદ્ર એનો
નહોયે કલંકી; બધું હોય જ ત્યાં સુપેરે.
ત્યાં પ્હેલી વાર વિરમીશ હું થાક ખાવા,
ભાથું ભરી નવલ ત્યાંથી સુરમ્ય બીજાં
શૃંગો નવાં અધિક ઉચ્ચ અપૂર્વ ભવ્ય
શોધીશ; ને નવ કદી જડશે મને તો
સર્જીશ હું નવનવોન્નત શૃંગપંક્તિ,
ને વિશ્વના પરમ અર્ક શું માનવીનું
હૈયું રમાડતી ધપીશ હું દિવ્યતામાં.

— ચંદ્રકાંત દેસાઈ

Chandrakant Patel

150-11 Reeves Ave., Flushing, NY 11367:writes Gujarati poems since many yrs.; Collection of poems "Youvan Khele Fag" published in 2001; his poems and articles were published in over a dozen of magazines and Newspapers; Editor of "Kalam" magazine of Gujarati Samaj of New York: in addition to writing, he is an Artist and Journalist too; by profession Mechanical Engineer working in The Defence Dept. of The U.S. Government; prominent and active member of The Gujarati Samaj of New York. He distinguished himself as a very successful organisor of many Kavi-Sammelans through Gujarati Samaj of NY, providing popular literary platform in the TRI-State (NY, NJ, Conn.) area, wherein eminent poets from India, USA and Canada were invited.

ફૂલોએ

પ્રવેશ્યો બાગમાં હું જ્યાં પ્રસારયું સ્મિત ફૂલોએ ;
ચમનની દોસ્તીની એ નિભાવી રીત ફૂલોએ !

નથી સ્હેલું જીવન જીવવું રહીને કંટકો વચ્ચે ;
રહીને બેફિક્કર ભારે, ભર્યું સંગીત ફૂલોએ !

ન કીધી લેશ કૈં ફરિયાદ ગુમાની વાયરા સામે ;
સ્વીકારી હાર, એ રીતે કરી છે જીત ફૂલોએ !

લૂંટઈ જઈ ખુદ, ગુલશનની જવાની જળવી કાયમ ;
સુગંધે બાગને રાખ્યો સદા સુરભિત ફૂલોએ !

હનીમૂન યુગ્મની સાખે સજવી રાતના રંગો ,
પડી ચરણોમાં ઇશ્વરનાં વધાવ્યું સ્મિત ફૂલોએ !

રૂપાળી પાંદડી પર હાથ જ્યાં અટકી ગયો ત્યારે -
સુગંધી વેરી દઈ મુજ પર વહાવી પ્રીત ફૂલોએ !

- ચંદ્રકાન્ત પટેલ

કોની આંખો ?

મેઘધનુષના રંગ લપેટી છલકે કોની આંખો ?
સકલ સૃષ્ટિની સુંદરતાથી ઝબકે કોની આંખો ?
શરમે એ તો જાય ઝૂકી, ને મૌન ભલે દેખાય ;
ફટાક દેશે જાત - સમર્પણ, ચાડી એવી ખાતી
          મીઠું મલકે કોની આંખો ?

ફરક ફરકે એવું કે ભઈ, ભલભલાની
          છાતી ફોલી ખાય !
ફાગણ ફોરી ટપક ટપકતી મટકે કોની આંખો ?
ખૂબ વેદના ભરી હશે, એવું લાગે જ્યારે
          રડી હશે એ આંખો !

કોણ જાણે એ સાચું ખોટું -
અણતાગી આ થાપ આપતી ચમકે કોની આંખો ?

શરાબનો મદભાર ભરેલી રમ્મતયાળી આંખો !
ફૂલ- ગુલાબી ફોરંતી આ ફરકે સ્ત્રીની આંખો !

- ચંદ્રકાન્ત પટેલ

Dr. Dilip Modi

C/o Mr. Kishore Modi, 130 New Road, Apt. K13, Parsippany, NJ 07054; medical practitioner (MBBS) over 25 Yrs. loves writing poems; published two collections of Ghazals and two collections of Muktaks covering about 1000 Muktaks.

હે, અમેરિકા ! (મુક્તકો)

હું સર્જવું છું અચંબો ભીતરે
દષ્ટિમાં મારી અમેરિકા ઠરે
કાર, રસ્તા, મોલ ને ગોરી ત્વચા
કોણ કોની કયાં કદી પરવા કરે ?

શિસ્તનું પાલન અહીંનો ધર્મ છે
ચોકસાઈ ને ચીવટ, શું કર્મ છે ?
સ્ફૂર્તિ ને ઉત્સાહ, જલસા ને ઉમંગ
પશ્ચિમી સંસ્કૃતિનો આ મર્મ છે

બસ અહીં તો ખાવું, પીવું ને મજા
ચોતરફ ફરકે છે ડોલરની ધજા
મુક્તિ, સુખ, સગવડ શ્વસું છું તે છતાં
હાંફું છું જાણે હું, આ કેવી સજા ?

આ ચલણ ગારબેજનું, આ ખાનપાન
શસ્ત્રના સોદાગરો, દુનિયા છે બાન
વર્ક, વેધર ને અહીં વાઈફ વિશે-

છે અકળ સઘળું, રહે સૌ સાવધાન
લાંચ-રુશ્વત કે ન છેતરપીંડી પણ
વૃતિ યે આદર્શ ને ઉત્તમ વલણ
કોઈ ચર્ચા કે દખલ ના કોઈની
સંયમોનું જોઉ છું વાતાવરણ

કયાંક કચરો-ગંદકી વર્તાય છે ?
કયાં ભિખારી પણ કશે દેખાય છે ?
ખૂબ ટ્રાફિક કિન્તુ અંધાધૂંધી નહીં
મન સુખદ આશ્ચર્યથી અંજાય છે

ખૂબસૂરત કોઈ ફૂલો જોઉ છું
આધુનિકતાનો હું ચહેરો જોઉ છું
આંખમાં મારી વસેલ રણમહીં
આજ ઘૂઘવતો હું દરિયો જોઉ છું

નગ્નતા આ દેશમાં છે
ભવ્યતા આ દેશમાં છે
સાહસો જીવંત છે સૌ-
વિદ્ધતા આ દેશમાં છે

-દિલીપ મોદી

Hasmukh Barot

Dy. Editor : Gujarat Times, 43 West 24th Street, 9th Floor, New York, NY 10010; writes Gujarati poems and short stories; has deep interest in literature as well as Gujarati, Hindi and Marathi Rangbhoomi (drama/plays); very active and prominent journalist for the last 20 years; worked as reporter, sub-editor and executive editor for many well known magazines and Newspapers and shouldered heavy responsibilities successfully.

માં, મને એવું કંઈ થાય....

સમી સાંજે ઘેનમાં ઘેરાતી મારી આંખડી
ઝબકીને મધરાતે જગે
રેશમી કમખાની કસ મૂઈ કસકસતી
વેરણ થઈ વાંસામાં વાગે !
મને લાગે, મારામાં કંઈ ઉગું ઉગું થાય...
માં, મને એવું કંઈ થાય...

સૈયરોની સંગાથે હું પાણીડે જાઉ
          તો ય મારગમાં એકલતા લાગે
આ પાદર, આ સીમ, આ શેરી, આ ગામ
મારી સામે સૌ ટગર ટગર તાગે !
મનનું પતંગિયું ક્યાં ઊડું, ક્યાં ઊડું થાય...
માં, મને એવું કંઈ થાય...

દર્પણમાં ચહેરો નીરખીને મારો
          હું જ મને ગમવા કેમ લાગું ?
આંખોમાં કાજળ આંજીને હું
          ખુદ મારાથી શરમાતી ભાગું !
આ શાની મહેકથી અંગ અંગ મારું મહેક મહેક થાય...
માં, મને એવું કંઈ થાય....

                                        -હસમુખ બારોટ

કનૈયાને આમંત્રણ

ગોકુળ ના આવો તો કંઈ નહિ, મોહન, તમે દ્વારકામાં રાસ રચાવજો
આખું વરસ છો વિસારી દો શ્યામ, એક શરદ પૂનમનાં તેડાવજો !

યમુનાના નીરનો મીઠો ઘૂઘવાટ હૈયામાં ભરી અમે આવશું
વનરાવનની મહેક ભરી રોમરોમ દ્વારકા નગરી મહેકાવશું
બની શકે તો શ્યામ ! પાદરમાં ચીતરેલા વૃક્ષો કદંબનાં મૂકાવજો !
                                          – ગોકુળ ના આવો તો કંઈ નહિ મોહન...

ગોકુળમાં શેનો વરતાયો અભાવ, ગોપ-ગોપીના હેતમાં શી લાગી કમી ?
છોડી મનભાવન ગોવર્ધનની માયા, તને સોનાની દ્વારકા એટલી ગમી ?
લીલુડા વાંસનો હાથ વેંત ટૂકડો લઈ એમાં ચાર-પાંચ છેદ મૂકાવજો !
                                          – ગોકુળ ના આવો તો કંઈ નહિ મોહન...

સાતે પટરાણીઓ સોળે શણગાર સજી રમવાને રાસ સંગ આવશે,
બીજું તો ઠીક, રાજની રાણીઓ રાધાનો ઉમંગ કયાંથી લાવશે
મસ્તકનો મણિ-મુકુટ અળગો મેલીને રાજજી!મોરપિચ્છ રૂડાં સોહાવજો !
                                          – ગોકુળ ના આવો તો કંઈ નહિ મોહન...

                                                    – હસમુખ બારોટ

ᏘᏘᏘᏘᏘᏘᏘᏘᏘᏘ

Dr. Indra Goohya

*126 Constituiton Drive, Orangeburg, NJ 10962; loves and writes poetry
since childhood, also writes short stories and plays; his first collection of
Gujarati poems was published in 2001; enjoys reading poetry in Gujarati,
Hindi, Urdu and English; Psychiatrist by profession. Enthusiastically
participates in Kavi-Sammelans and presents Ghazals effectively.*

'લ્યા, તું જ જાગને !'

કરવો છે એક સવાલ આ ફેલાતી આગને,
પહેરો ભરી રહ્યાં એ સીસમને ને સાગને.
જો હોત પાનખર તો કોઈ પ્રશ્ન ના થતે,
કોણે વસંતમાં આં ઉજાડયો છે બાગને !
આવ્યો સમય છે કેવો કે ખૂદ ઈશ્વરે કહ્યું,
'આપી શકું તને હું કંઈ એવું માગને !'
ખાબોચિયામાં જે કદી ડૂબી ગયા હતા,
નીકળ્યા છે આજ લેવા દરિયાના તાગને !
અસ્થિર પૃથ્વી કેમ છે, લાગી રહ્યો છે શું ?
માણસના પાપનો જ ભાર શેષનાગને !
ભેરી લઈ હું નીકળ્યો સૌને જગાડવા,
લોકો એ સાંભળી કહે, 'લ્યા, તું જ જાગને' !

– ઈન્દ્ર ગુહ્ય

ᏘᏘᏘᏘᏘᏘᏘᏘ

★ તારા ગામમાં

છો હોય તારા આશકો અનેક તારા ગામમાં,
એ અનેકોથી વધુ હું એક તારા ગામમાં.
ક્યારેક ચોરાઈ હતી આ દિલ તણી સઘળી મતા,
જે શોધતા નીકળ્યું પગેરું છેક તારા ગામમાં.
ને દોષ દેવાને મળ્યો શું હું જ આખરમાં તને ?
મુજ સિવા સૌ હોય જાણે નેક તારા ગામમાં !
નવપ્રણયની ધૂપદાની લઈ ઘૂમીશું આપણે,
ચોતરફ ફેલાઈ જશે મ્હેક તારા ગામમાં.
તું કહે તો છોડશું સંસારના બંધન બધાં,
પણ જોગી થઈને જગવશું અહાલેક તારા ગામમાં.
એ દિવસ નક્કી તને પણ યાદ મારી આવશે.
કાન પડશે મોરલાની ગ્હેક તારા ગામમાં.
પગ નહિ ઊપડે ભલે પોકાર તું, 'પાછા ફરો',
તુજ ગામ તજવાની લીધેલી ટેક તારા ગામમાં.

– ઈન્દ્ર ગુહા

★ ૧૯૮૧માં અમેરિકા આવવા મુંબઈ કાયમ માટે છોડ્યું ત્યારે લખેલી ગઝલ

Indra Shah

577 St. Lawrence Str., East Lake, OH 44095; Lawyer, writes Gujarati poems, sometimes English too; published one Guj. Poetry Collection; conducts Kavi-Sammelans; ex-partner in The Weltman, Weinberg and Reiss Law firm; past president of FICA and editor of its News letter; Trustee of Cleveland and Cuyahoga Bar associations; Secretary of Ohio State bar Association; Recipient of President's Award, Freedom Award and Asian leadership Award from various Ohio Organizations; Chairman, Community Relations Board, Ohio; Chairman, Asian Advisory Committee, Amer. Red cross, Ohio; Chairman, Outreach Committee, Lake Country Rep.Party.

ખાલીપો

ભરચક ભીડ વચ્ચે ધ્યાનસ્થ બેઠો હોય છે ખાલીપો.

કોલાહલથી તેનેં વ્યર્થ ભરવા મથું છું.

હું જ્યાં જાઉં ત્યાં– –

લગ્નમાં, પાર્ટીમાં, સિનેમામાં, નાટકમાં, સંગીતમાં

પડછાયાની જેમ પીછો કરે છે એ.

ઊંઘમાં પણ મને એ છોડતો નથી.

છળી ગયેલા બાળકની માફક

મને વળગીને એ

સૂઈ જાય છે મારી પડખે આખી રાત.

ત્રણ કાર ગરાજ અને પાંચ બેડરૂમના

ઘરને સંપૂર્ણ રીતે તે ભરી દે છે

અને તેને હું અણગમતા અતિથિની

જેમ વિદાય આપવા ઈચ્છું છું.

પણ નવજાત શિશુની માફક

રાતે ન વધે તેટલો દિવસે

અને દિવસે ન વધે તેટલો રાતે

તે વધે છે, વધે છે,

વિસ્તરે છે, વિસ્તરે છે

અને આખો અવકાશ તેનાથી ભરાઈ જાય છે.

અને પછી તે અજગર બની મને

ચારે બાજુ વીંટળાઈ વળે છે; મને ભીંસે છે;

હું હવાની જેમ તેને કાપવા મથું છું

શબ્દોની ધારદાર તલવારથી

ચોતરફ ઉમટ્યું છે

આ ખાલીપાનું પૂર

ગોઠણ સુધી, ગળા સુધી

માથાનીય ઉપર

ઘેરી વળ્યું છે મને

અને હું ડૂબું છું, ડૂબું છું, ડૂબું છું.....

– ઈન્દ્ર શાહ

એક તાઓ-ગઝલ

માછલી માફક અનાયાસે તરું સ્વભાવમાં
જીવું પણ સ્વભાવમાં અને હું મરું સ્વભાવમાં

પવન લઈ જાય જ્યાં ત્યાં પર્ણ વહી જાતું
તું લઈ જાય ત્યાં જાઉં અને વિચરું સ્વભાવમાં

વિચારો મને લઈ જાય છે ગતને અનાગતમાં
સ્થગિત થૈને 'અહીંને આ ક્ષણે' ઠહેરું સ્વભાવમાં

અભિવ્યક્ત થાતું શબ્દમાં તે તો કદાપિ સત્યના
અતલ આ મૌનના ઊંડાણમાં ઉતરું સ્વભાવમાં

અક્કડ હશે તે તૂટશે પણ અમે ઝૂકી જશું
જગત આખું ભલે જીતે હું હાર સ્વીકારું સ્વભાવમાં

– ઈન્દ્ર શાહ

Jalendu Vaidya

105 Fornelius Ave. Clifton, NJ 07013; writes poems, novel and short stories for many yrs. ; participates in poetry readings, takes active interest in Indo-American Lit. Academy's meetings; published Novel "Tarasu" and a collection of short stories "Purva Janma"; by profession Civil Engineer and Astrologer.

સત્ય

પથરાં તો ઠોકરે ભાંગતાં તૂટતાં રહે
પિગળવાનું પૌરૂષ તો પાષાણ પાસે જ છે.

ફૂલડાં તો મોસમે ખીલતાં ખરતાં રહે
અંગારને પ્રાણ કરવાનું તો પર્ણ પાસે જ છે.

ઝાંઝવા તો જીવને લોભાવી છેતરતાં રહે
તૃષ્મિનું તારણ તો વીરડાં પાસે જ છે.

વસંત તો વૃક્ષોને વર્ષ ઘરડાં કરે
તાપણાંનું તર્પણ તો શિશિર પાસે જ છે.

ભણેલાં તો કારકૂનમાંથી માંડ મહેતા બને
કમાવવાનું કૌવત તો કબાણ પાસે જ છે.

કાવ્યો તો વંચાઈને ભૂલાતાં વિસરાતાં રહે
જીવતરનું જેમ તો કહેવત પાસે જ છે.

પ્રેમ તો પાંગળો પળમાં પલટ મારી જય.
સંબંધ સાચવવાનું સામર્થ્ય તો વિશ્વાસ પાસે જ છે..

- જલેન્દુ વૈદ્ય

Jayant Desai

4 Darien Ct. Apt. 1D, Pomona, NY 10970. He writes poems since his college days, he likes to draw sketches and has interest in fine Arts. He possesses keen interest in Yogasadhana and conducted Yoga Camps in India. He is Engineer by profession (B.E. Civil from M.S. Univ.) and lives in USA for the last 13 yrs.

એમ્નેશિયા★

સૂક્કાં, ખરેલા પાંદડાઓને
કચડતો સમય ચાલી જાય છે,
નિર્વિઘ્ન, નિર્ધ્વનિ,
વગડાને વીંધીને, સડસડાટ...
ઓટાતા સૂર્યની સોનેરી ગોધૂલિમાં
આળોટતા પાદરને એકાએક ખરીઓ
ફૂટી નીકળે છે અને
મનના ઊંડાણોમાં અંકુરાતું ગોવાળિયાપણું
ફસફસતા ફીણની જે ઉભરાઈ ઢોળાઈને
શમી જાય છે....

ઘેરા રંગમાં પલોટાતું જતું તળાવનું પાણી
મારા લટાર મારતા પગો, કિનારેથી ઉતરડાતી-
ખરતી ધૂળ અને વાતાવરણમાં ઘૂંટાતી
ગમગીનીનો તાળો મેળવવા
એકટકી લગાવીને જંપી ગયું છે...
અંધારાને પણ વજન હોય છે,
એનો અનુભવ અને એ માટેની ઉંમર,

બંને અત્યારે એકીસાથે મારા પર તોળાઈ
રહ્યાં છે ત્યારે મારી સુક્કી-કાચની લખોટીઓ જેવી
આંખો મને અસહાય બનીને કટકે કટકે તૂટતો જતો
જોયાં કરે છે, તદ્દન નિર્ભાવ-નિર્લેપ બનીને...
–હજી આવીને પૂરાં પાંગરે
એ પહેલાં જ ટૂંપાઈ ગયેલાં શૈશવ, કૈશોર્ય
અને મૌગ્ધ્યને હવે કેટલીય રાતો પંપાળી,
મનાવી-પટાવીને ચૂપ કરી દેવાં પડે છે...
દોસ્ત, પ્રેતાત્માઓ કરતાં ય વધારે ભયાનકતા
પ્રશ્નાર્થો પેદા કરી શકે છે અને
આટોપાતા શ્વાસની સાથે ય, ઉપર હવામાં
મંડરાતાં 'કાશ' ચેડાં કરી શકે છે...
પાછો ફરું છું ને પગ નીચે દબાઈ ગયેલું
ઘાસ ફરી ઉભું થતું જોઈ શકું છું.
અરે જસ્ટ એ...ના, ના !!
હવે મને બીજું કશું જ દેખાતું નથી, સદીઓથી
પણછ ખેંચી ઝાડ પરના પંખીને જોઈ રહેલા
મારામાંના પેલા અર્જુન સિવાય..!...!!....
બાકીના બ..ધા...કૌરવો, દ્રોણો, પાંડવો....
આ વગડાને એકીટશે જોઈ રહ્યા છે...
અને ?....!!!વગડાને વીંધીને, સડ...સડાટ
સૂક્કાં, ખરેલાં પાંદડાઓને કચડતો
સમય ચાલી જાય છે, નિર્વિઘ્ન-નિર્ધ્વનિ...

★સ્મૃતિક્ષય

– જયન્ત દેસાઈ

Kanu Gajjar (Bindu)

5315 Huntingfield Drive, Mississauga, Ontario, L5R 2G2, Canada; living in Canada for 30 yrs.; writes poems since many years; worked as Artist in Toronto for 10 yrs.; as journalist in Gujarati "Sabras" magazine; Interior designer for Banquet halls and Restaurants; published collection of Children songs; worked as political Cartoonist for Gujarat Herald; his paintings were exhibited in many states in India; prepared murals for movie theatres and Gujarat Govt.; acted in dramas too.

તડકાને આંજ્યો છે આંખમાં

કે આજ મેં તો તડકાને આંજ્યો છે આંખમાં.

વરસાદી વાદળામાં ઝૂલતી સવાર ને
ખૂશ્બૂમાં તરબતર ધરતી.
ભીના આ તડકાની સુંવાળી કાયામાં
દેખું હું મહેંકને નીતરતી

સૈં, મારી આંખ્યુંની અંદર ના ઝાંખ મા.
કે આજ મેં તો તડકાને આંજ્યો છે આંખમાં.

ઝાડવેથી તડકાને વીણવાની મોજને
માણું મારા દલડાની સંગે.
ટહુકાઓ ભીના થઈ વળગ્યા છે જેને
કેવા મધમધતી અવનીને અંગે.

મેર મુવો વાયરો ય વળગીને બેઠો કાખમાં
કે આજ મેં તો તડકાને આંજ્યો છે આંખમાં.

- કનુ ગજ્જર (બિન્દુ)

એકાકી

ધોબીના શાપ થકી ભટકતી બાળ છું,
નાનકડી દુનિયામાં રહીસહી ભાળ છું.
જમેલી સદ્‌ગત સ્મૃતિઓની ધૂળ છું,
સૂકાભંઠ ફૂલો સાથ શેષ રહી શૂળ છું.
થાકીને જંપી મારી ભવ્યતાની વારતા,
અવાવરૂ કૂવાની તરસીલી પાળ છું.
મારી આ દુનિયા, મારી ના થઇ શકી,
ઠરેલા જ્વાળામુખીની હૈયા વરાળ છું.
સહરાના તાપમાં નિરવતા ભોગવું,
પગલાને પામવા, તત્પર પરસાળ છું.

- કનુ ગજ્જર (બિન્દુ)

Kishor Raval

7901 Henry Ave. # G 109, Philadelphia, PA 19128. He considers himself as a prose person and frequently writes short stories and sometimes poems too; Lymeric style poems are his favourite. He had toyed & developed a tool to write Gujarati on computer, which he has popularized by now. For the last six years he is the editor of the bi-monthly magazine on the internet named Kesuda (www.kesuda.com) rich in short stories, poems & articles with beautiful pictures in water colors. He is computer programmer by profession and retired since six years. He lives in USA since many years.

સાથિયો

પ000 વર્ષ પહેલાં પૂર્વજોએ
માનવીનાં સૌ સુખ અને ઝંખનાઓને
ચાર ખાનામાં ગોઠવ્યાં,
ધન-ધાન્ય, ઘર-બાર, આરોગ્ય અને સંતતિ.
કોઇ ગ્રાફિક ડિઝાઇનરે
તેને એક સરળ, સુંદર, આકૃતિમાં મૂર્તિમંત કરી
અને સાથિયો સર્જ્યો !

તો ભલા મને એ તો સમજાવો કે
એક હિંસક પશુએ
તેની કલગી કરી માથામાં નાખી અને
અસંખ્ય, અસહાય માણસો પર અત્યાચાર કર્યો
તો
એમાં સાથિયાનો શો વાંક?
એ બિચારો કેમ દંડાય?

માનવજાત પડછાયાને ભસવાનું બંધ કરશે ખરી?

– કિશોર રાવલ

Dr. Kishore Modi

130 New Road, Apt. K-13, Parsippany, NJ 07054; lives in USA for the last 12 years; writes peotry since many years; he has often participated in All India Radio programs; published three collections of Ghazals; writes all kinds of poems in Gujarati including Chhand, Achhandas, Sonnets, Hiku, Tripadi etc.; possesses Ph. D. in Science; he worked as Research Officer at Sarabhai Research Centre and worked as Consultant in the field of Chemistry; at present he works as manager at the Concord Laboratory in New Jersey; published five books on the life of great scientists; his research papers have been published in various science journals; Institute of Chemists, Calcutta honoured him as the Fellow of The Institute; his name appeared in The Who's Who of the Commonwealth.

શબ્દ શબ્દમાં

બારાખડી ગજવી છે મેં શબ્દ શબ્દમાં,
ખુદ જાતને જગાડી છે મેં શબ્દ શબ્દમાં.

આ ભાલ પર કરચલીઓ વિસ્તરતી જાય છે,
ને ગોઠડી મળાવી છે મેં શબ્દ શબ્દમાં.

કંઈ જાણકારી તારી શેરીની મળી નહીં,
ઘર બારણે ચગાવી છે મેં શબ્દ શબ્દમાં.

ગઝલોના અર્થમાં ઘણી સંભાવના મળી,
ચાહીને ક્ષણ સજાવી છે મેં શબ્દ શબ્દમાં.

સૂઝબૂઝ છે જ ક્યાં જગતમાં તે છતાં કિશોર
કૈં ગૂઢતા વધાવી છે મેં શબ્દ શબ્દમાં.

– કિશોર મોદી

ઈશના રૂપે

સહુ એટલે મને જુએ અવહેલના રૂપે,
પથ્થર છું કેમ થઇ જ્યારે ઈશના રૂપે.

આજીજી શીદને કરીએ આપણે હવે?
સઘળું મળે છે એકધારું ઝંખનારૂપે.

વરસોથી કેટલી મહેનત ચાલુ છે હજી,
કે હું મને ઝબ્બે કરી દઉ ચાહનારૂપે.

માયા ઉશેટી ક્યાં જવું એની ખબર નથી,
મૃત્યુની એક વાત છે સંભાવના રૂપે.

એકાંતમાં મને ઝુરાપો બહુ ગમે કિશોર,
મારે પ્રકટવું છે ગઝલમાં વેદના રૂપે.

— કિશોર મોદી

Kundan Patel

C/o. Days Inn, 610 US Route 1 North, Edison, NJ 08817, writes poems since many years; Lata Mangeshkar has sung her songs & its audio Cassettes are available; owns and manages Days Inn.

ધરતીનો.... સંતાપ....

સહસ્ર શૂળે કંપી ઉઠી
       ધરતી... માતા... આજે
કુખે જન્મ્યા બાળક એના
       અંદરો અંદર બાઝે
કોને કેમ કરી સમજાવે !
       એની વિમાસણ છે ભારે...
એક બીજાની સાથે રમતા
       એક જ ભાણે સાથે જમતા
શાને બન્યા લોહી તરસ્યા
       શાની કાજે બાઝે ?
કોને કેમ કરી સમજાવે !
       એની વિમાસણ છે ભારે...
ખિલ ખિલ સૌની સાથે હસતી
       ગજ ગજ એની છાતી ફૂલતી
શાને આવી વિપરીત ઘડી
       શાને અકારા... લાગે ?
કોને કેમ કરી સમજાવે !
       એની વિમાસણ છે ભારે....
સપૂત જન્મ્યા એની વધામણી
       કપૂત પાક્યા એવી અભાગણી
દૂધની ધારા સુકાઇ ગઇ તે
       વેરણ રાતો.... લાગે
કોને કેમ કરી સમજાવે !
       એની વિમાસણ છે ભારે....

- કુંદન પટેલ

Manu Naik

63, Richard Drive, Dumont, NJ 07628; worked as Engineer in USA for the last 35 years and recently retired; loves writing Gujarati poems, specially Chhand & Sonnets.

નાની બાળાનો સાથિયો

(મંદાક્રાન્તા)

પ્હેલી વેળા કુસુમ વરણી એક બાળા લહી મેં
મમ્મી સાથે હઠ પકડતી સાથિયો પૂરવાને
મમ્મી આપે વિવિધ નવલાં રંગ તે આંગળીએ
વ્હેતા મૂકી જળકમળના સાથિયાને પખારે

નાના હાથે મુખ કમળને ટેકવી એક ચિત્તે
રંગો પૂરી કમળદળની પાંખડીને સજાવે
તેની મમ્મી મધુ મરકતી નેણમાં વ્હાલ દીપે
આવ્યા જાણે સકળ સુખ ત્યાં રંગ ભીની સવારે

ધીમે વ્હેતા પરિમલ ભર્યા વાયુની સાથ તેના
જુલ્ફાં કેરી અલક રમતી તે હવે થાક ખાવા
આવી ઊભી મૃદુ હલકથી નેણ સામે જરા ત્યાં
જોતી રૂડા નયન મુકુરે રંગ બે સાથિયાના

કીધી તેણે અલક અળગી રંગની આંગળીએ
ને ભાલે ત્યાં જળકમળના રંગની બ્હાર કૂદે
કૂદે જાણે સરલ સરતી વ્યોમની વાદળીના
રંગો રાતાં કમળદળની ખીલતી પાંખડીમાં

તેના ભાલે લલિત રમણો સાથિયો જે બન્યો તે
ચૂમી લેવા મન તલસતું જાણું ના તોય તેને !

– મનુ નાયક

રેસ્ટ ઇન પીસ, મધર ટેરેસા !

મધર ટેરેસાએ
વાદળીના ચાર ખૂણે
ચંદ્રકિરણની દોરી બાંધી.
અને
દોરીના બીજ ચાર છેડા
તારાની ખીંટી પર વીંટી
વાદળીની ઝોળી બનાવી.
પછી તેણે
મોટાં મોટાં શહેરમાં
કે નાનાં નાનાં ગામડાંમાં
જેની ભ્રૂણહત્યા થઇ છે તેવી
ઉકરડા પર ફેંકેલી
બાળકીને ઝોળીમાં મૂકી
ધીમે ધીમે ઝુલાવવા માંડી.
આમ કરતાં કરતાં
તેના ગળામાં
ડૂમો એવો ભરાયો કે
તે હાલરડું ના ગાઇ શકી
એટલે બાળકી બધી રડવા લાગી.
પણ અલ્ટ્રા-સાઉન્ડ મશીનમાં
ખણખણ થાતા રૂપિયાના
રૂપેરી અવાજમાં
અને

પોતાની પિપૂડી વગાડતા
લોકોના મોટા શોરમાં
તેમનું રુદન સંભળાતું નથી.
''રેસ્ટ ઇન પીસ મધર ટેરેસા !''
આવું કહેનારાને
ખબર પડશે ખરી
કે મધર ટેરેસાને
શાંતિ મળી નથી !

- મનુ નાયક

Dr. Minaxi Patel

14 Hamilton Drive West, North Caldwell, NJ 07006; writes poems since many years; active member of Santh Din-Poetry reading group; received Ph.D. by writing thesis on Dhumketu's short stories; lives in USA for last 25 years; works as teacher at the Dikinson High School of Jersey City for the last 20 years.

બે મારા - બે તારા

કોઇનાં સૂના આભમાં ઉગ્યા
પ્રેમના ચાંદ-સિતારા
હાલ્યને ગોરી વીણવા જઇએ બે મારા બે તારા
ઝમતી રાતે મહેંકી ઉઠ્યાં
મોગરા પારીજાતક
હાલ્યને ગોરી વીણવા જઇએ બે મારા બે તારા
સંધ્યા ટાણે સાગર તળિયે
મોતીડાંના હારા
હાલને ગોરી વીણવા જઇએ બે મારા બે તારા
દરિયાની વેળુમાં ખૂંચ્યા
છીપલાં વળી શંખ
હાલ્યને ગોરી વીણવા જઇએ બે મારા બે તારા
હળના ચાસે મૂળિયાં ખુલ્યાં
બાજરીયાના દાણા
હાલ્યને ગોરી વીણવા જઇએ બે મારા બે તારા.

- મીનાક્ષી પટેલ

શબોને બોલવું છે

પડેલાં શબોને બોલવું છે
પોતાની પહેચાન ખુદાને આપવી છે
નથી ગાયના છાણનો ચોકો
નથી ગંગાના જળનું આચમન
નથી ક્રૉસનું મોમાં મૂકાવું કે
નથી કુરાને શરીફનું વાંચન !
અરે,
શ્વાસ લેવાની પણ જગા નથી
એવું કેવું આ
સમશાન કે કબ્રસ્તાન !
અલીને દાહ દીધો છે
ને
રામને દફ્ન કીધો છે
છતાં યે
શબો સૌ શાંત સૂતાં છે
નથી યે આંગળી ચીંધી
નથી યે લાકડી લીધી
ભાઇચારાનું આ સ્વર્ગ
મર્યા પછી અમોને લાધ્યું છે
શબોને બોલવું છે
માનવીની પહેચાન ખુદાને આપવી છે

- મીનાક્ષી પટેલ

Nalini Gandhi

P.O. Box 451064, Atlanta, GA 31145; writes poems since childhood; her poems published in Gujarati & other magazines; participates in literary & social events; Engineer from V.J.Tech. Inst. Bombay; lives in USA for last 32 years.

હાશ !

ધગધગતો તડકો,

        મળે લીમડાની છાંયડી; હાશ !

સખત ગરમી અને ઉકળાટ

        વરસાદનું ઝાપટું; હાશ !

કડકડતી ઠંડી અને હિમવર્ષા

        લાડકાનું તાપણું; હાશ !

ઘનઘોર ઘેરાયા નભની ક્ષિતિજમાં

        સૂર્યનું કિરણ; હાશ !

આફતોનાં પહાડ વચ્ચે ગુંચવાયા પંગુને

        કેડીનો માર્ગ મળે; હાશ !

બાટલીના બુચ સમો ડૂમો જ્યાં રુંધતો

        પળનો એ શ્વાસ મળે; હાશ !–

વર્ષોના વિયોગ પછી મળવાની ઝંખના,

        પ્રેમનું આલિંગન; હાશ !

- નલિની ગાંધી

અંગત સંબંધ

તવ છબી સમીપે દીવો કર્યો'તો મેં,
              શ્રદ્ધાનું તેલ આવી પૂરી ગયા તમે !

મોટી ભયની દિવાલો ચણી'તી મેં,
              મુજ ડરપોકતા છાના ચોરી ગયા તમે !

અહંકારનું રૂપ ઓઢ્યું'તું મેં,
              આયનામાં ઇશ પ્રતિબિંબ દેખાડી ગયા તમે !

જૂનું નિર્બળતાનું ઘરેણું પહેર્યું'તું મેં;
              શક્તિનો નવો ઘાટ ઘડી ગયા તમે !

આંખોમાં આંજ્યુ'તું અજ્ઞાનનું આંજણ મેં;
              પરમજ્ઞાનની લાલી ગાલે લગાડી ગયા તમે !

નિરાશાનાં ચીર વીંટ્યા'તા મેં,
              હતાશાનું વસ્ત્ર-હરણ કરી ગયા તમે !

ચિંતાઓ ઘણી સંઘરી'તી દિલમાં મેં,
              મુજ દાબડીમાં આત્મવિશ્વાસ ભરી ગયા તમે !

કોઇ નહોતું ને બારણું અડકેલ્યુ'તું મેં,
              મુજ સાથે અંગત સંબંધ બાંધી ગયા તમે !

– નલિની ગાંધી

Dr. Natvar Gandhi

14625 Stonewall Drive, Silver Spring, MD 20905. He writes poems-mostly sonnets in Gujarati, since many years. His collection of sonnets has been recently published. He is the recipient of the Vishva Gurjari Award for his outstanding work in the field of Tax & Finance. He is working as the Chief Financial Officer of the Govt. of the District of Columbia. He is Ph.D. in the field of Finance.

જૂના વતનથી

જૂના વતનથી પ્રવાસી જન આવતાં જે કહે:
વસો અહીં શું સાવ ઉભડક આમ ઊંચા જીવે?
ભવિષ્ય ભૂલી વર્તમાન જીવતાં, ત્રિશંકુ તમે,
અહીં નહીં, નહીં તહીં, સતત કેમ વ્હેરાવ છો?
તજી જનની, જન્મભૂમિ, ધનની ધુરા ખેંચતાં,
વિદેશ વસતા કુતૂહલ સમા, અહીં કોણ છો?
અહીં સ્વજન કોણ છે? અકરમી મટચા હિંદના.

જરૂર તજી હિન્દની સરહદો, પરંતુ મટચો
નથી જ નથી હિન્દી હું, તજી નથી જ એ સંસ્કૃતિ
કદી બૃહદ હિન્દની, નથી ભૂગોળ પૃષ્ઠે, ભલા,
સીમિત કદી ભવ્ય ભારત, વળી સવાયો થઇ
અમેરિકન, હું થઇશ ગુજરાતી ગાંધી તણો,

સહિષ્ણુ સમુદાર નાગરિક હું બનું વિશ્વનો,
સદૈવ, રટું મંત્ર એક : વસુધૈવ કુટુમ્બકમ્

- નટવર ગાંધી

એમિલી ડિકિન્સન

પ્રવેશ કરવા દઇ સ્વજન, મિત્ર બેચાર ને
સલાક જડબે તું બંધ કરી બારી ને બારણાં
વિષાદમય જીવતી જીવન કલાંત એકાંતનું
સૂની કુહરમાં, અનૂઢ, ઉરભગ્ન, એકાકિની.
દુવાર સહુ બંધ તોય જન કૈંક આવી વસે,
પુરાઇ ઘરમાં છતાં ભમતી ભવ્ય ભૂલોકમાં,
તરે તું ઉરગર્ભના અતલ ગૂઢ પાતાળમાં,
દઇ ડૂબકી લાવતી મણિ સહસ્ર મુકતાફળો.

વિદાય થકી પામતી મરમ સ્વર્ગ ને નર્કના,
કદીક મરતી કરે કવન કબ્ર, કૉફિનનાં,
સવારી લઇ આવતા મરણ દૂત અદ્ભુતના,
અનંત જીવિતવ્યના, જખમ સૂક્ષ્મ, વૈફલ્યના.

કવિ તમસ, તેજની, પ્રવણ સત્ય, સંક્ષિપ્તની,
અનામી, કદી નમ્ર તો, કદીક ઉગ્ર, વિદ્રોહિણી.

- નટવર ગાંધી

Dr. Nilesh Rana

1531 Buck Creek Drive, Yardley, PA 19067. He writes poems since many years. His poems appeared in several magazines. His one Novel & one collection of short stories have been published. He is Medical Doctor by profession and lives in USA since 34 years.

ડૉક્ટર

શ્વેત ચાદર તળે કંપતું ક્ષીણ શરીર
હાંફતા શ્વાસને ઑક્સિજનનો ટેકો
નાડીમાં મંદ પડતી ગતિને ધીરેથી ધક્કો મારવાનો
બાટલીમાંના લાલ પ્રવાહીનો મરણિયો પ્રયાસ....
અધખુલ્લી પાંપણે અટકેલું અપંગ જીવન
હોઠો પર આથમતો અસ્પષ્ટ અવાજ
બોઝલ બોઝલ એક પ્રશ્નનો પ્રસવ
ખુલ્લી હથેળીમાં તરસતી રેખાને
ધીમેથી ઉષ્મા ભરેલ હાથોથી દાબી
ચૂપકેથી દરવાજો બંધ કરી
બહાર નીકળતાં....
માથા પર અચાનક એક ટપલી.
જોયું પાછળ વળી તો...!
ખડખડાટ હાસ્ય વિખેરતા મૃત્યુનો સવાલ
'મજાક કરે છે, તું પણ મારી જેમ'
આંગળી ચીંધી મેં
'સાયલન્સ પ્લીઝ'ની તકતી તરફ
અને કહ્યું
'અહીં બોલવાની મનાઇ છે'
અને.....

– નીલેશ રાણા

ધુમ્મસની ધાર

આજ મને વાગી ગઇ ધુમ્મસની ધાર,
તોય મને દેખાતું બધું આરપાર.

સ્થળને ને જળને મેં વ્હેરાતાં જોયાં
ને જોઇ લીધું પળપળનું તળિયું,
ગોપી એક સંગોપી બેઠી છે કયારની
વ્હાલમનું વૃંદાવન ફળિયું.
મારા હોવાની ભાવના સંભાવનાથી
આપું નિરાકારને હુંયે આકાર.

વ્હાલમના વાઘાનું લિલામ કદી થાય નહીં
ને મોરપીંછનાં મૂલ નહીં અંકાય,
વાંસળીના સૂરને ઝીલવા હું જઉ
ત્યાં યમુનાનાં વ્હેણ આ વંકાય.
તારી ભુજમાં હું ભીંજતી ભૂંસાતી
હવે જોઇએ નહીં કોઇનો આધાર.

– નીલેશ રાણા

Niranjan Bhagat

99, Lavendar Lane, Rocky Hill, Ct. 06067; Eminent top ranking poet of Gujarat & India; published seven poetry collections in Gujarati & English; Recipient of Ranjitram Goldmedal, Narsinh Mehta Award, Sahitya Academy Award & many others; writer of eight volumes of critical study of Indian & world literature; ex-professor of English literature at St. Xeviers College, Ahmedabad, India.

ભિખારી

આ હાથ જે સામે ધર્યો
એ હાથને ઘડનારનો પણ હાથ
એના જેટલો લાચાર ને પામર ઠર્યો,
ત્યાં કોણ કોને આપશે રે સાથ?
કરશે કોણ કોની બંદગી ?
આ વણહસ્યે ગુજરી ગઇ છે જિંદગી,
એમાંય હસવાનું મને એકાદ તો જે કે મળ્યું બ્હાનું,
પ્રભુનો કેટલો તે પાડ માનું?
કહો તમે એણે ઘડ્યો આ હાથ
જેણે આ જગત સરજ્યું?
જગતનો નાથ
કહી છો? આ જ ને એનું જગત કે હુંય તે જેમાં વસું?
ને તે છતાં જો 'ના' કહો તો નહીં હસું.
'હા' તો તમે ક્યાંથી કહો? જ્યાં હાથ મેં સામે ધર્યો
તેવો જ તે નન્નો સર્યો !
પણ ચન્દ્રસૂરજતારલા
હું ગ્મા હથેલીમાં રમાડું, કોઇ તો આપો ભલા !
જે કેમ હું ક્યારનો એમાં વહું છું કેટલાયે ભારને,
સૂનકારને.

- નિરંજન ભગત

ઑરોડ્રોમ પર

આ વિહંગ,
શું વિરાટ, તીક્ષ્ણ તેજ, સ્નિગ્ધ અંગ અંગ;
શી પ્રલંબ ફાળ !
પર્ણહીન વૃક્ષની અહીં વિશાળ ડાળ
તે પરે કરે વિરામ, તે ક્ષણેય પાંખ તો પ્રસારતું,
વિહાર વેગવંત દૂર ઓ.... સુદૂર,
ઊડવું જ ઊડવું, ન ધૈર્ય ધારતું;
ન નીડમાં, નભે જ ગીત ગાય એકસૂર;
સ્હેલતું, સદાય સ્હેલતું,
પરંતુ શું સુભાગ્ય કે ઇંડું ન મેલતું !

– નિરંજન ભગત

Nita Dave

3124 Shadetree Dr. Mississauga, Ontario, L5N 6P3, Canada; writes poems since many years. Her poems published in many magazines; writes short stories & articles too; actively participates in literary activities & Kavi-Sammelans; organizes programs of eminent writers & poets; lives in Canada for 13 years; possesses B.S. & M.S. in Microbiology & Analytical Chemistry, also Business Management Diploma; works as interpreter / translater.

સંભવામિ યુગે યુગે...

એ લોકો કહે છે કે એ વાતને
લગભગ પાંચ હજાર વર્ષ થવા આવ્યા છે
પણ તમે ખરેખર માનો છો કે
એ વાતને પાંચ હજાર વર્ષ થવા આવ્યા છે?

જો એમ જ હોય તો કેમ આ
રોજેરોજ ચીરહરણ થતા દેખાય છે?
હા, વાત તો સાચી જ હોવી જોઇએ-
કારણકે દુ:શાસન અને દુર્યોધનનાં ચહેરા
સાવ ધૂંધળા થઇ ગયા છે.

પણ આ શું?
થોભી જાઓ...
એ ધૂંધળા ચહેરા એકાએક કંઇક
ચોક્કસ આકાર પામી રહ્યા છે -
એમાંથી કંઇક સ્પષ્ટ દેખાઇ રહ્યું છે -
અરે,
આ તો અર્જુન અને કૃષ્ણ !!

- નીતા દવે

Panna Naik

*9034 Lykens Lane, Philadelphia,PA 19128; eminent poet and writer;
published seven collections of poems; recipient of Chunilal Mehta Literary
Award; worked as librarian in USA for many years; actively participates
in literary activities; teaches Gujarati in Univ. of Penn.*

કૂર્માવતાર

અહીં અમેરિકામાં
નિવૃત્ત થયેલી
વૃદ્ધ થતી જતી વ્યક્તિઓની આંખમાં
એક જ પ્રશ્ન ડોકાયા કરે છે :
– હવે શું ?
ભારત જઈ શકાય એમ નથી
અમેરિકા રહી શકાય તેમ નથી
સંતાનો તો ઊડીને સ્થિર થઈ ગયાં
પોતપોતાના માળામાં અમે બધાં
સિટી વિનાના સિનિયર સિટીઝન.
અમે છાપાં વાંચીએ
– પણ કેટલાં ?
અમે ટેલિવિઝન જોઈએ
– પણ કેટલું ? ક્યાં લગી ?
સ્થિર થઈ ગયેલો સમય
અસ્થિર કરી મૂકે છે અમને
– અમારા મનને.
સસલાં અને ખિસકોલીની જેમ
દોડતો સમય
અચાનક કાચબો થઈ જાય ત્યારે
એ અવતારને શું કહેવાય ?

– પન્ના નાયક

꧁꧂

માતૃભાષા

આપણને
જે ભાષામાં સપનાં આવે
એ
આપણી માતૃભાષા.
મને
હજીય ફિલાડેલ્ફીઆમાં
સપનાં
ગુજરાતીમાં આવે છે.
પણ
મારી આસપાસના
ગુજરાતીઓ
ઉમાશંકરની છબિ જોઈને
સતત પૂછયા કરે છે :
'આ કોની છબિ છે ?'
અને
મારું સપનું નંદવાઈ જાય છે.
(સપનાંનાં હૈયાંને નંદવામાં વાર શી ?)

- પન્ના નાયક

Pravin Patel (Shashi)

80 Corona Ct.,old Bridge, NJ 08857; writes poerty in Gujarati and sometime in English too;writes fiction (novels and short stories), inspirational nonfiction;published two poetry collections, 5 novels, 2 collections of short stories & one nonfiction collection of his Articles;published poems, articles, short stories in over 15 magazines; recipient of honourable mention for his English poem 'Metamorphosis' by New Jersey Poetry Society, New York - Governor, New York -Mayor and President Bush appreciated this poem; writes popular column "Wah American Wah" in Gujarat Darpan magazine for the last 9 yrs. prominent active member of The Indo-American literary Academy;Postgraduate in Accounts, Business, marketing, Finance, labour Management and works as Controller in New Yorker Law firm;lives in USA for last 25 yrs.

આગબંબાવાળાની પ્રાર્થના

ગમે ત્યાં આગ ભડકી ઉઠે,
અને મને ફરજ ઉપર બોલાવવામાં આવે,
કોઈ દૂજની જીંદગી બચાવવા
પ્રભુ મને તું શક્તિ દેજે.

મોડું થઈ જાય તે પહેલાં
નાના બાળકને હું બાથમાં લઈ લઉં,
અને કોઈ વૃદ્ધને ઉંચકી
ભયાનક આગમાંથી ઉગારી લઉં.

આગ લપકોને ઠારી શકું
યાચું બળ મોત સામે લડવા,
નાનો અમથો સિસકારો સાંભળી શકું
સદા મને સજાગ રાખજે.

વિશ્વાસ ના ડગે આડોશી-પાડોશીનો
માલમતા એમની સલામત રાખું,
ના થાઉ ફરજ ચ્યૂત કદી
લગાવી દઉં જનની બાજી.

તકાજે કાળનો અગર હોય
બીજાને બચાવતાં ખપી પણ જાઉં,
માંગું એટલું હું તારી પાસે
તારૂં સદા મને શરણ મળે.

- પ્રવીણ પટેલ (શશી)

અલવિદા !

અસ્ત થાય સૂર્ય જ્યારે
અને મારા જીવન પંથનો અંત આવે,
નથી જોઈતી ધર્મવિધિ
અને શોકાતુર રૂદનખંડ ત્યારે,
રડો શા કાજે
જીવ તો સંચર્યો અનંતની વાટે.

સાલશે ગેરહાજરી
અને વિસારે પડી જઈશ જ્યારે,
રહેજો આનંદ મગ્ન
અને સંભાળજો સુખદપળો આપણી ત્યારે,
રડો શા કાજે
જીવ તો સંચર્યો અનંતની વાટે.

નિશ્ચિત છે યાત્રા
અને જવાનું ચોક્કસ છે દરેકે,
ખેલ આ બધો નિયંતાનો
બુલાવો એનો લઈ જવા ઘેર એને,
રડો શા કાજે
જીવ તો સંચર્યો અનંતની વાટે.

યાદ મારી તમોને આવે
અને હૃદય ઉભરાઈ જાયે,
જજો આપણા મિત્રો પાસે
અને દાટી દેજો ઉદાસી, સંકલ્પો સાથે,
રડો શા કાજે
જીવ તો સંચર્યો અનંતની વાટે.

- પ્રવીણ પટેલ (શશી)

Pravin Vaghani

4 Fiona Crt., Glen Waverley, Vic 3150, Australia; writes poems and articles for many years; honorary editor of ("Matrubhasha" Bimonthly); very active in promoting Gujarati Language and its literature.

જરૂર હોય છે

જગતમાં જે કાંઈ છે તે બધું
એક બીજા માટે છે.
ઈશ્વરને ય વિધાતા થવાને
મનુષ્યોની જરૂર હોય છે.
નથી શણગારાતા ફૂલોથી
બગીચા, કાંટાળા વૃક્ષો વિના.
અત્તરના એક ટીપા માટે
સેંકડો ફૂલોની જરૂર હોય છે.
શાંતિની મહત્તા શું સમજે
જેણે નથી ભોગવી વ્યથાઓ.
અનુભવવા સુખની પરાકાષ્ટા
દુઃખી થવું જરૂરી હોય છે.
ભટકે છે કંઈક વટેમાર્ગુઓ
નિરુદ્દેશના જંગલમાં
સિદ્ધિને રસ્તે ચાલવા
મંઝિલની જરૂર હોય છે.

અનાથો જે હોય ના તો
કોણ આશ્રયદાતા બની શકે?
થવા દાનવીર ધનિકોને
ભિક્ષુકોની જરૂર હોય છે.
ન થશે કોઈ ધનવંતરી જે
કોઈ બીમાર હોય ના
પ્રખર કથાકારને પણ અબુધ
શ્રોતાઓની જરૂર હોય છે.
સેંકડો ઝરણા ઠલવાય ત્યારે
એક સરોવર ભરાય છે.
ઘટાદાર વૃક્ષને પણ લાખો
પાંદડાની જરૂર હોય છે.
પ્રવીણ ખોટા ઉજાગરા કર મા
ભવિષ્યની ચિંતામાં,
વિધિના લેખ સમજવા
શાંત નિદ્રાની જરૂર હોય છે.

- પ્રવીણ વાઘાણી

Preetam Lakhlani

65 Falcon Drive, West Henrietta, NY 14586; writes poems, articles, short stories since many years; published four collections of poems and three books of short stories and articles; edited two collections of Gujarati poems and two collections of short stories, both from Indo-American poets and writers; lives in USA for last 26 years; possesses Master Degree and works in the computer field.

અસ્તિત્વ

નજર પરોવી

બધું જ જોઈ શકું છું

સૂરજનું એક કિરણ લઈ

બારી ઉઘાડું

એકમેકની આંખમાં.

આ શહેર

કશોક વિરફોટ સર્જવા

તરસ

સ્પર્શ

એકાંત

વૃક્ષોની ઘટામાં ઘેરાતું

મારી આંખોની સામે જ ઓગળે.

સમયની દિવાલે ઝુલતા

અરીસામાં

માણસનું સરનામું
ધુમ્મસના દરિયામાં
હિલોળા લીધા કરે.
પોતાનું અસ્તિત્વ
ખોઈ બેઠેલો માણસ
વરસાદી સાંજે
ટિટોડીના સ્વરે લસરતો
વિવિધ સ્વરૂપે
એક ઝાંખી-પાંખી ક્ષણ પકડવા
અદૃશ્ય થઈ જાય.
લાલ લીલો સમય
હસ્તરેખામાં ઊઠતો વંટોળ
પછડાત ખાતો
ઊભેલાં ઠુંઠા વૃક્ષો પર
ઝરમર ઝરમર વરસે.
તરસ નામે જગી ઊઠે
પૂછડી નામે પટપટાવતા
પુષ્પોના રંગો
ખોવાયેલ માણસને શોધવા
સ્વપ્નની આંગળેથી !!!

- પ્રીતમ લખલાણી

અતીત

અતીતની ગુફામાં
ઊભો છું
આંખો બંધ કરીને
આભાસી આવરણો
કશુંક ખખડવાનો અવાજ
અજગર થઈને સરકે
રેશમના મખમલી તાંતણા
ભીતરની આગ પર
ચંદનનો શીતળ લેપ કરે
લહેરી ઊઠે રોમ રોમ...
ખરતા રહ્યા
ઉમંગો અને ઉત્સવો
ક્યાંય સુધી શ્વાસમાં
ઘરની દીવાલ
લીલું મૌન થઈને છવાય જય
બારણાંની ચૂપકીદી
લીમડાની ગંધમાં આળોટે
મીંચી રાખેલ આંખો
ખોલું છું
ક્ષણ માટે
ઝળઝળતા દર્પણ
ગોખે ટમટમતા અસંખ્ય દીવા !
પહાડ, નદી, ઝરણાં અને દરિયો
ધરતી આભ વચ્ચેનો સેતુ
ચોમેર કેવળ આનંદ !
ઉત્સાહની પાંખેથી ખર્યા કરે
વેરાયા વિના ચારે કોર....

– પ્રીતમ લખલાણી

Preety Sengupta

*15, Stewart Pl., Apt. 7E White Plains, NY 10603; M.A. (English Lit.);
living in USA for last 35 yrs., Eminent poet and writer, writing since
Childhood; published 31 books comprising Poetry and world-travel reminding
great travel writer Kaka Kalelkar, she has her own literary style; Received
several Awards from Gujarati Sahitya Academy and Gujarati Sahitya
Parishad of Gujarat; Received Vishwa Gurjari Award for being the first
Indian travelling to North Pole; She was Vice President of The Gujarati
Literary Academy of North America; her poems and articles regularly
published in reputed magazines and awarded prizes too.*

બાણશય્યા

વાદળાં ભેગાં થાય છે ને ગાજતાં નથી.
દરિયાને તળે કોઈ મોતી
ફરી એક ટીપું થવા ઝંખી રહે છે.
તગતગ થતું ટીપું
જેમાં ઊભા થાય સ્મિતના શીશમહેલ.
કોઈ કિનારો છોડે છે,
પણ મઝધારથી દૂર રહી જાય છે.
કોઈ તળેટી મૂકે છે,
પણ શિખર સુધી પહોંચતું નથી.
શ્વાસોના હાંફથી જ અંતર
અંતર મપાતું નથી.
જે ઉકેલ છે તેને કોયડો થવું છે,
સીધુંદોર છે તેને ગાંઠે વળવું છે.
પ્રવાસ ચાલુ રહે છે, રસ્તો કપાતો નથી.
ભીષ્મની પીડા મને સમજાય છે.
લોહી ઝમ્યા કરે છે, તીર વાગતાં નથી.
પાણી ટોળે મળે છે, પૂર આવતાં નથી.

- પ્રીતિ સેનગુપ્તા

ગંગોત્રી

આકાશે વાદળ નહીં, ના કોઈ પંખી ઊડે,
તીક્ષ્ણ-તીવ્ર પાષાણ શૃંગો કાળકર્કશ ;
ભીષણ, ભયાનક, ભૈરવ-વરણ
લાગે બીભત્સ ધવલ-ચારુ હિમ-આલિંગને.
શીત-સ્તબ્ધ લઘુનદીઓ
      મલિન, ધૂલિગ્રસ્ત જે
થઈ રણકઝણક ઝરણ વહી આવે નીચે–
ધૂલિગ્રસ્ત પર્વતીય પ્રાચિરો વિષે.
ના ઝાડ, ઘાસ કે ઝાંખરાં,
ના જીવ કે જીવન કશું.
બસ, એક મસ્ત મહાસરિત
ધસમસી રહે આરંભના ઉન્માદમાં.
એની ગતિ, એની ગીતિ,
ગર્જરમુખર રવ-મોહિની.
દશ્ય, શ્રાવ્ય, આસ્વાધ ને
મનને કરે મંજુલ, સભર.
આ જ જીવિત પૂર્ણ, આમાં
અર્થ જીવનનો બધો.

– પ્રીતિ સેનગુપ્તા

Rajni Parikh

1 Rushton Ct. Princeton Junction, NJ 08550; writes Gujarati poems since his High school period; his poems have been published in many reputed magazines, actively participates in Kavi-Sammelans and literary activities; Chemical Engineer by profession; president of the Chemical Firm in New Jersey, selling chemicals; lives in New Jersey since many years.

'અંતરીક્ષમાં વસતા પિતાનો સંદેશ'

મારી છબિ પાસે આવી, આંસુ ના વહાવો,
હું અહીં રહેતો નથી, 'હું સફર કરું છું'.
ખેતરમાં હિલોળતા મોલ પર હિંચકું છું,
વસંતના વાયરામાં હું ઉડ્ડયન કરું છું.
પ્રથમ વર્ષાની સૌરભમાં પ્રસરું છું,
પુષ્પ ક્યારીઓને હું સુશોભિત કરું છું.
ચાંદની રાતમાં શીતળતા અર્પું છું,
આકાશના તારલિયા ને હું પ્રકાશિત કરું છું.
કોયલ ના ટહુકારમાં ગુંજન કરું છું,
બાળકોના વદન પર હું હાસ્ય કરું છું.
પહેલા તમે મારા હ્રદયમાં રહેતા હતા,
હવે તમારા હ્રદયમાં હું નિવાસ કરું છું.
મારી છબિ પાસે આવી, આંસુ ના વહાવો,
હું અહીં રહેતો નથી. 'હું સફર કરું છું'.

- રજની પરીખ

Dr. Ramesh Kanojia

9 McGovern Ct.Bridge Water, NJ 08807; writes poems since his Highschool years, mostly Chhandobaddh and has good knowledge of Pingal Shastra; fond of reading Gujarati and Sanskrit poetry; his poems published in many magazines; participated in poetry readings in many Kavi-Sammelans in Tri-state area; he possesses degrees from Bombay University and Ph.D. in Medicinal Chemistry from The University of Wisconsin; he worked as Research Scientist, also as principal Scientist and Research Fellow in The Drug Discovery Division of Johnson and Johnson Pharm. Company in New Jersey for many years; he has at his credit over 60 scientific publications and patents and several prestigious Research Awards of JNJ Corp.; recently retired and willing to devote more time to poetry.

વિર્સજન અને નવસર્જન

(શિખરિણી)

પ્રવાતો, આંધીઓ, પ્રલયપૂર, વંટોળ, વિફરો,
ઘુમો વિશ્વે વૈશ્વાલન અતરપ્યો ખાક રચતો,
હિમાદ્રી શૃંગેથી પ્રબળ ઉમટો પુષ્કર ઘનો,
પ્રકોપી પિનાકી સજી ત્રિશુળ સંહાર સરજે !
મિનારા, મ્હેલાતો જરજરીત ખંડેર પલટચાં
સ્મશાનો સર્જાણા, ઘરઘર ચિતાગ્ની પ્રજળતાં,
સુપુત્રી વંઝા થૈ, સકલ પરિવારે ઉઝડતાં,
સૂની સૃષ્ટિ શોકે, નયન નીર નિર્બંધ નીતરે !
વીતી સંધ્યા, રાત્રિ, અનિલ શીત સંજીવની બને,
હવે શૃંગે, ખીણે, નવજીવન ઉલ્લાસ પ્રસરે,
સુશોભે સેંથીમાં નવવધુ ઉષા સુર્ખ ભરતાં,
પ્રકાશે સસ્મિતે, રવિકિરણ સૃષ્ટિ સજીવતાં !

(શાર્દૂલવિક્રીડિત)

સંધ્યા રાત્રિ પછી ઉષા બની જતી, અંધાર તેજે ઝગે !
સાધે સર્જક સર્જના વિસરજી, સૃષ્ટિ રચે શૂન્યથી !

- રમેશ કનોજીઆ

ચેરી-બ્લોસમ

(અમેરિકન વસંત)

પતઝડમાં ઉજ્જડ જે સૃષ્ટિ, મૃતવત, શીત, સૂતી શાંત શિયાળે,
નવજીવન ઉલ્લાસ પ્રસારે, જલ, થલ, પવન, વસંત વહાણે !

સજીવન થઈ પંખી કલરવતાં, કલકલ ઝરણ સંગીત નિનાદે,
ભમરાનાં ગુંજન, ચુંબનથી, તરુ રૂંવે કૂંપળો, કુસુમકળી વિકસે !

'ડૈફોડિલ્સ' પિતાંબર પહેરી, કવિજન મન રીઝી કાવ્ય સુઝાડે,
રંગબેરંગી 'ટ્યુલિપ્સ' તો રાજા, મનહર વિવિધ ફૂલોમાં વસંતે !

નદીવટ 'વોશિંગટન' નગરીમાં, ધવલ એ 'ચેરી-બ્લોસમ' ધનવને,
'કુસુમાકર ઋતુરાજ હું' ગુંજત, ફૂલ, ફૂલ નિરખ્યા મેં શ્યામ વસંતે !

-રમેશ કનોજીઆ

Ramesh Shah

10 Liberty Ave. Apt. 2L, Jersey City, NJ 07306; writes poems, plays, short stories and Novels; he has published one collection of poems, one collection of short stories and six collections of Akanki plays; also three long plays, 110 TV-scripts; worked as actor and director in his own plays; recipient of four Gujarati Sahitya Academy Awards for his plays, Batubhai Umarvadia award and his one novel received award from Guj. Sahitya Academy; worked as professor in Ahmedabad for 26 yrs.; presently lives in USA and active member of Santh Din poetry Group.

સૂફીવાદી ગઝલ

અંતરમને કોનાં નૂપુર કૈં રણઝણે ?
ઝૂલી રહ્યા મદહોશના બસ પારણે !

જઈને કહો કે આંખ મીંચે ના જરા,
લટકી રહ્યા એની નજરના તાંતણે !

છે કોતર્યું ઝાકળ પર એનું સ્મરણ,
ઊડી ગયું, ઊગ્યો સૂરજ એ કારણે !

પ્રેમનાં પુષ્પો બધાં ચરણે ધર્યાં,
યાદો સુગંધિત ઝૂરતી આ આંગણે !

થૈ પ્રેમવશ પ્હોંચ્યા અમે ઉત્તરધ્રુવે,
પાછાં ગયાં દસ્તક દઈને બારણે !

ચાહત અમારી લોક છોને નિંદતા,
શાયર પછી ગાશે ગઝલ સંભારણે.

— રમેશ શાહ

નિર્હસ્તક

બંધ મુઠ્ઠી ખોલું છું...
કશું જ નથી મારા હાથમાં !
એમ તો ક્યાં કશું હોય છે હાથમાં ?
કોણ ક્યારે ક્યાં હોય છે સાથમાં ?
બાથમાં લેવા મથું છું,
પણ છટકી જાય છે...
હવાની જેમ...અફવાની જેમ...ખોવાવાની જેમ !
અને રહી જાય છે હાથ ખાલી !
સાલી, આ કોણ દે છે હાથતાલી ?
એ જ રમવાની સતત સાતતાલી !
કોઈ સંતાય ને કોઇના માથે દાવ,
મને મૂકી દીધો છે દાવમાં-
ત્યારથી હું દોડું છું...પકડવા મથું છું...
પકડાતું નથી કશું જ !
બધું જ અદૃશ્ય.. ઈશ્વરની જેમ !
બધું જ દૂર... આકાશની જેમ !
નિરંતર બધું...સમયની જેમ !
કેમ કશું કંટ્રોલમાં નથી મારા ?
કશી જ હોતી નથી મારા હાથની વાત !
મારો જન્મ થયો એમ જ

ને શરૂ થઈ ગયું જીવન...
નખ વધે છે આપોઆપ,
વાળ ખરે છે રાતોરાત
ટાલ પર હાથ ફેરવી શકું છું
એટલી જ મારા હાથની વાત !
બગાસું આવે છે એમ જ
ઈવન છીંક પણ મારી ઈચ્છા વિનાની !
કોઈ ખેંચે છે ઊંચે આસમાન તક-
તાકે છે ટગર ટગર કાળની જેમ !
ક્ષણે ક્ષણે ઘસડાઉ છું એ તરફ-
કરું છું કર્મ, કર્તવ્યના ભાવથી
અને અભિમાન લઈને ફરું છું !
ને કશું હોવાની હથેલી ધરું છું, બસ !
બધું જ બંકસ, બબાલ
નિરર્થક, નથીંગ, નિર્હસ્તક !
કારણ કે -
જન્મથી જ
મેં મારો હાથ ગુમાવી દીધો છે !

- રમેશ શાહ

Randhir Naik (Magna)

356 Burgess Place, Clifton, NJ 07011; writes poems since many years; his collection of poems will be published very soon; active member of Santh Din poetry group; actively participates in Kavi-Sammelans of Tri-state area.

ચહેરા

ઉદાસીનાં મહોરાં પહેરી ફરતા ચહેરા
સ્વાર્થના બુરખા ઓઢી મળતા ચહેરા,
દર્દ ફરિયાદ અને મતલબ પૂરા થયા
લાગણીને લાત મારી ખસતા ચહેરા.
ભીંત બારી બારણા પોપચાં ઢાળતા રહ્યા
સ્મૃતિના રૂમાલે અશ્રુ લૂછતા ચહેરા.
ઉંબરા વરંડી કે પાદરની યાદ વાગોળી
સ્પર્શની મીઠી ભીનાશે હસતા ચહેરા.
દુવા દવા અને પ્રાર્થના ફીઝ થઈ ગયા
હવે શ્રદ્ધાની ચ્યુંઇંગમ ચાવતા ચહેરા.
કલાકો દિવસો ને વર્ષો વીતી ગયા
માદરે વતનની યાદે ભિંજાતા ચહેરા.

- રણધીર નાયક

શું શું ગયું...

ટોડલો, ઉંબર, બારી, બારણા ને પછી શું શું ગયું
પાદર, ખેતર, સીમ, ફળિયા ને પછી શું શું ગયું
તરફડે છે જીવ એકલો ડોલરિયા ખંડેરમાં
શબ્દ, અર્થ, મૌન, ધારણા ને પછી શું શું ગયું
પ્યાસાને ભલા અહીં પૂછનાર કોઈ જ ના મળે
નહેર, તળાવ, નદી ઝરણાં ને પછી શું શું ગયું
પાણી જરા ટેહલવા નીકળ્યું બેસીને નાવમાં
હોડી, હલેસા, દરિયો, તરણા ને પછી શું શું ગયું
ટેરવે હજી ચોંટી રહી છે વતનની ધૂળ
શહેર, રસ્તા, ગલી, આંગણા ને પછી શું શું ગયું.

– રણધીર નાયક

Dr. Rasik Pandya

4613E Desert Sands Drive, Chandler, AZ 48249; he writes poems since 50 years; published two collections of poems and a book of tribute to his father, which includes poems & articles; he is a Medical Practitioner and worked as Health officer for many years in various Municipal Govt. in India; he lives in USA for the last 25 years. and worked at the New Jersey Hospital for several years; he belongs to a family of eminent poets in Gujarat.

હડસન નદીના કિનારે

એક હબસીની છોકરી તરવાને આવી હડસન નદીના કિનારે;
અડધાં પાણી લાગે કાળાં ને ભૂરાં હબસણના સાપણ સેલારે.
કઠે ઊગેલું લોહ-સિમેન્ટનું વન જ્યાં રાની પશુના ઘૂઘવાટા,
મોજાંના ફીણની ઉજિયારી ઝાંયમાં સાન ને ભાન ઘૂમરાતાં;
ખીણ અને પ્હાડમાં માછલાંની હોડદોડ અડતી ના એને લગારે.
હડસન નદીના કિનારે.

સંતાકૂકડી રમે પુષ્ટ અંગ પાણીમાં, સ્વિમીંગ-સ્યૂટે ના સમાતાં,
વાદળાંની આડશથી સૂરજ દે તાલી વાયરાનાં રોમ થાય રાતાં;
ઊભરાતી કાયા તે બાર કે બત્રીસની, કહેવું બત્રીસીને ભારે.
હડસન નદીના કિનારે.

કાળા ભમ્મર કાળીનાગથી ય કાળા વાળની ફણા-ફેન શોભે,
હડસેલે હડસેલે હડસનનાં હડકાયાં પાણીનું ઝેર જય મોભે;
હાથ-પગ એવા તે વીંઝોટે કાળવી કોરાં કેં કાળજાં ભીંજ્યા રે.
હડસન નદીનાં કિનારે.

પાણી ફીણે ને જય એમાં મઢાઇ, જાણે કોઇ જલની પરી,
પાણી પાણી થાય તાકી તાકીને આંખ, સરકે અરી ને પરી,
હડસન થઇ જય ક્યાંક કાલિન્દી કાળા ને ધોળાના નેણને ઇશારે,
હડસન નદીના કિનાર.

- રસિક પંડ્યા

બટુક ગિરિ આ

(મંદાક્રાન્તા)

નાનો મારો બટુક ગિરિ આ સ્વપ્નનો સાથી મારો
દૈનં દિને નજીક સરતો વાસ્તવોનો કિનારો
જોવાની ના જરૂર પડતી ના ખસે આંખમાંથી
જોવી છોડું છત સદનની ડોકતો કયાંક કયાંથી.

વ્હેલી પ્રાતે પઠન કરતો તારકો કેરી પોથી
ઝોકાં ખાતો પલક મુજપે; સૂર્યનાં રશ્મિઓથી
જાણે કોઇ છવિ ચીતરતું હોય પૂંઠે રહીને.
એવો તો એ નીખરી ઊઠતો, આવતો શું નહીને.

તો પ્રાવ્રુષે જલદ જૂથના ધૂમ્રગોટે મઢેલો
રાતા પીળા અગન રસનો ઊછળે જેમ રેલો
જોયો સૂર્યોદય સમયમાં ક્ષિતિની પાર્શ્વભૂમાં
ખાલી થાતાં સહજ બનશે ચાલવાનું ય લૂમાં.

જોતાં જે ના ધરવ વળતો, રમ્ય કેવો અનુપે !
જાણે બીજું નયન મુજ એ પ્હાડ સન્ટેન રૂપે.

— રસિક પંડ્યા

Sarla Vyas

412 Orlando Street, Edison, NJ 08817; she writes short stories, novel, essays & poems; her writings are published in several magazines & news papers in USA & India; published one book of collection of short stories based on her experiences of Indians trying to settle down in American life; her Novel is recently being published continuously every month in popular "Gujarat Darpan"; she is a very active member of the Indo-American Literary Academy and participated in many poetry readings of the Academy; she worked in India as Higher Secondary School teacher for many years; at present she works & lives in USA since many years.

આંસુડાં જીવાડે

હું જન્મ્યો ને સારવા લાગ્યો આંસુ
બદલો વાળ્યો મેં નવમાસ કેદનો,
જીવન મળ્યું છે જીવવાને માટે,
આંસુ સારતો રહ્યો હું જીવનની વાટે,
જિંદગીના દુ:ખો સહ્યાં આંસુઓથી,
સુખમાં સરી પડ્યાં હર્ષનાં આંસુ.
પરાજય માં વહેતાં રહ્યાં આંસુ.
જીતની ખુશીએ પણ સરી પડ્યાં આંસુ
પ્રગતિએ છલકાઇ રહ્યાં આંસુ
મારી અધોગતિમાં સરી પડ્યાં આંસુ
પ્રિયજનના વિરહે વરસ્યાં આંસુ
પ્રિયજનના મિલને સરી પડ્યાં આંસુ
ક્રોધમાં આંખોથી ઝરતાં રહ્યાં આંસુ
કરુણાએ હૃદય પીગળી સરી પડ્યાં આંસુ.
મિત્રની મિત્રતાએ વરસ્યાં હેતનાં આંસુ
વેરીના વેરથી સરી પડ્યાં આંસુ
આંસુ મારી જિંદગી, આંસુ મારી બંદગી,
જન્મનાથ આંસુ મૃત્યુનાથ આંસુ
આંસુ એ જ જીવન, જીવન એ જ આંસુ.

- સરલા વ્યાસ

ત્સુનામી ! તારા પાપે

એ કાળરાત્રિએ
જાણે ત્રિલોચને
ખોલ્યું ત્રીજું નેત્ર
અને શરૂ કર્યું
નટરાજે તાંડવ,
ધરતી લાગી ધ્રૂજવા
પાતાળનાં તળ ફાટ્યાં
ને ડહોળાવા લાગ્યો દરિયો,
જાણે શેષનાગે માર્યો ફૂંફાડો.
વિફરેલા દરિયે માઝા મૂકી
ઉછળ્યા તરંગો તાડ ને આંબવા
તાણી ગયો દરિયો સૌને,
કોઇનો ભરથાર, કોઇનો ભાઇ,
કોઇની પ્રિયા તો કોઇની બહેની,
કોઇનાં મા-બાપ તો કોઇના બાળ,
બન્યા બેઘર લોકો ચારેકોર,
વેર્યો વિનાશ દરિયે ધરતી પર
ભયભીત થઇ કંપી રહ્યાં
લોકો કુદરતના આ કોપે.
ઝુંપડીના એક ખૂણે
ભયથી કાંપતી બાર વર્ષ
ની બ્હાવરી બાળા

ચિંથરે હાલ, વિયોગે
મા-બાપના, સારી રહી આંસુ.
કાળ બનીને આવ્યો,
નરપિશાચ એક
દયા બતાવી બાળાને
હાથ વાંસે ફેરવી રહ્યો;
બાપ જેવો માની બાળા
બાઝી એને, રડી રહી.
સામે દરિયે માઝા મૂકી
અહીં પિશાચે માઝા મૂકી
કુમળી કળી શી લાચાર બાળા
બેઘડી હૂંફ પામી રહી
ત્યાં તો એણે બચેલાં
ચીર પણ ચીરી કાઢ્યાં
ચિત્કારતી રહી બાળા
કર્યો કૌમાર્ય ભંગ બાળાનો
બુઝાવી કામની આગ નરાધમે,
તરફડી રહી બાળા
આંખો એની ફાટી,
દેહ નિશ્ચેતન બની રહ્યો,
જીરવી શકી વિયોગ મા-બાપનો
અસહ્ય બન્યો આ આઘાત એને.

- સરલા વ્યાસ

╺◖◗╸◖◗╺◖◗╸◖◗╺◖◗╸◖◗╺◖◗╸◖◗╺◖◗╸

Shailesh Desai

3124 Shadetree Drive, Mississauga, Ontario, L5N 6P3, Canada; writes poems since many years; articles too; his poems published in many magazines; actively participates in literary activities & Kavi-Sammelans; organizes programs of eminent writers & poets; lives in Canada for 13 years; possesses B. Pharm & Diploma in Business Management; works as Pharmacist in Canada.

એક નોર્થ અમેરિકન બાળકની આત્મકથા

મારો જન્મ એ કિશોરાવસ્થાનો
એક અકસ્માત
ગર્ભપાતવિરોધીઓનો વિજય
ને પછી અકસ્માતોની ઘટમાળ....
મારું ભવિષ્ય નક્કી કરનારા,
ધોળા અને કાળા કોટવાળા,
ફોસ્ટર પેરન્ટસ્ કે પછી
અનાથાલય અને ન્યાયાલય
આ બધી ઘટનાઓમાં ક્યાંક
મારા Biological parents આવી જાય
સાથે ય આવે કે પછી છૂટા છૂટા,
એમના સંજોગ પ્રમાણે.
અને પછી પ્રવેશ થાય
'કહેવાતી' Surrogate Mother નો;
આ બધી ઘટનાઓને અંતે
હું કદાચ ફરી બે મા જ વાળા
કે ફક્ત બે બાપવાળા ઘરમાં
પણ જઈ શકું.

- શૈલેશ દેસાઈ

╺◖◗╸◖◗╺◖◗╸◖◗╺◖◗╸◖◗╺◖◗╸◖◗╺◖◗╸

ઉકો

મારું નામ ઉકો
જન્મ ૧૯૨૫, ૧૯૩૫ કે ૧૯૪૫
જન્મ સ્થળ : રામપુર કે મિરઝાપુર
કે પછી ડેલહાઉસી
તમને જે ગમે તે....
સમય જતાં... કદાચ ૧૯૪૭ માં
સમજ જતાં કે પછી સમજ આવતાં
આઝાદી આવતાં કે આઝાદી જતાં
ગમે તે હોય પણ
મારું નામ યુસુફ થયું
પછી સમય જતાં, ન ઉકો, ન યુસુફ રહ્યો
અને થયો જોસેફ
પછી ડૉક્ટર, એન્જિનિયર
કે ચાર્ટર્ડ અકાઉન્ટન્ટ થયો
અને થઇ સાલ... ૧૯૮૫, ૧૯૯૦ કે
પછી ૨૧મી સદી
અને પેસિફિક કે એટલાંટિક પાર કર્યા
એમ જ કહો.. બે ચાર કે
સાત સમંદર પાર કર્યા
અને પછી... અટકી પડયાં
ન અર્થ સર્યા,
જોસેફ, યુસુફ કે ઉકાના નામોથી
આ બધું રંગાયું છે અહીં
ચામડીનાં રંગોથી.

- શૈલેશ દેસાઈ

⁊⁊⁊⁊⁊⁊⁊⁊⁊⁊⁊⁊⁊⁊⁊⁊⁊⁊⁊⁊

Shakur Sarvaiya (Shabab Kayami)

He is a pharmacist and lives in USA since many years ; writes Gujarati peoms in Achhandas, Geets & Ghazals; he has one collection of his poems published.

કસમ છે, બસ કરો

આંખ બંધ થઇને જગતી હોય. છે,
નજરને નજર પણ લાગતી હોય છે.
હું મર્યો અર્થને શોધતાં શોધતાં,
સમજણો જિંદગી માંગતી હોય છે.
જ્યોતિષો ચડભડે ક્યારના જાણવા,
ભીંતમાં શું તરડ શોધતી હોય છે.
કોઇના સ્મરણના રકત આ દદદડે
યાદ પણ ખંજરો રાખતી હોય છે.
એ કથાને કહો કેમ પૂર્ણ કરવી?
જે પૂરી થઇ છતાં ચાલતી હોય છે !
કસમ છે બસ કરો, ના ભરો આહને શબાબ,
ડુંગરે ભેખડો તૂટતી હોય છે.

- શકુર સરવૈયા (શબાબ કાયમી)

નથી સરળ

ડૂબેલા સૂર્યને રોકવાનું છોડ તું,
હાથમાં પવનને પકડવાનું છોડ તું;
કતલ મારી જશે થઇ બીક એવી છે મને,
ઘાસને બેધડક કાપવાનું છોડ તું;
એકલા એકલા ભટકવાનો શ્રાપ છ,
લે જુદાઇ હવે બાંધવાનું છોડ તું;
કોઇ આ ફીણમાં જિંદગી મારી હશે,
ચમકતા બુદબુદો ફોડવાનું છોડ તું;
એક આગ બળતી ભીતરમાં ક્યારની,
ઉપરથી રાખને ફૂંકવાનું છોડ તું;
બુદ્ધ થાવું નથી સરળ જેવું ધારતો શબાબ,
ઝાડની ઓથમાં બેસવાનું છોડ તું;

– શકુર સરવૈયા *(શબાબ કાયમી)*

Subodh Shah

32 Oakmont Terrace, East Windsor, NJ 08520; he writes poems in Gujarati, English & Sanskrit; also writes serious prose in English; knows many languages: Gujarati, Hindi, English, Marathi & Sanskrit; he has almost finished a book in English encompassing the critical study of India's cultural problems, which will be published soon; he is a scientist having wide experience in research & development in Applied Chemistry.

ગુડ મૉર્નિંગ

ગુડ મૉર્નિંગ, અમેરિકા !
આર્ટિફિશિયલ ઇન્ટેલિજન્સ,
જનીન દ્રવ્યો ને જીન્સ
વર્ચ્યુઅલ રિઆલિટી
બ્લૅક હોલ્સ ને બ્રાઇટ બ્રેઇન્સ !

ગુડ મૉર્નિંગ, ભારત !
સાંઇબાબા, અજમેરી બાબા,
અરે ! કંઇ કેટલા બાબા ?
રથયાત્રા, કુંભમેળા,
શંખનાદી શંભુમેળા
બ્લૅક બૉમ્બ્સ ને બ્રાઇટ બ્રેઇન્સ !

– સુબોધ શાહ

હાયકુ

શ્વાની વિયાઇ
સાત વાર; જટાયુ
હજી વાંઝિયો.

સો સો કૌરવો
અક્ષૌહિણી અઢાર
અર્જુન એક.

વરુ સંહારે
ઘેટું બકરું; નહીં
સિંહ, ના વાઘ

- સુબોધ શાહ

⛧⟐⟐⟐⟐⟐⟐⟐⟐⟐⟐⟐⟐⟐⟐⛧

Sudhakar Bhatt

157-34 23rd Ave. Whitestone, NY 11357; he writes poems since last 10 years and participates in poetry readings of Indo-American Lit. Academy and kavi Sammelans; he is the son of well known poet of a popular poem "Ekaj de Chingari", who lived with Mahatma Gandhi in Sabarmati Ashram for 10 years; In memory of his late father he published collection of his father's poems, which was inaugurated by well knwon Indo-American writer Madhu Ray; he is M.S. (Civil Eng.) and worked as Civil Engineer with New York City's Transit Authority for 30 years.

જીવનનૈયા

હે પ્રભુ મુજ તારણહાર
જીવનનૈયા પાર ઉતાર
તુજ દયા છે અપરંપાર
તું જ છે જીવન આધાર.... હે પ્રભુ
ઘોર ભર - અંધકારમાં
વમળવચ વીંટળાઇ ગયો
દિશા કયાંય દિસે નહીં
મનોમન મૂંઝાઇ ગયો... હે પ્રભુ
ન દિસે મારગ મારો
ન દિસે જવાનો આરો
તુજ વિના આ જીવનનૈયા
કયારે પાર થવાનો વારો ?... હે પ્રભુ
પાય લાગી વિનવું આજે
તુજ દયા યાચવા કાજે
જ્ઞાનગંગા વહાવ આજે
જીવનનૈયા તારવા કાજે... હે પ્રભુ

- સુધાકર હરિહર ભટ્ટ

⛧⟐⟐⟐⟐⟐⟐⟐⟐⟐⟐⟐⟐⟐⟐⛧

Sudhir Patel

7504 Double Springs Ct., Charlotte, NC 28262. He writes Gujarati poems, mostly Ghazals since many years. His two collections of poems have been published. His poem was awarded first prize in the Gujarat Times poetry competition. His poems appeared in two Anthologies and several magazines. He is Accountant by profession and lives in USA since many years.

રાત થોડી, વેશ ઝાઝા

જલ્દી કરજે આવવામાં, રાત થોડી, વેશ ઝાઝા.
વાર નૈ લાગે જવામાં, રાત થોડી, વેશ ઝાઝા.

દશ્યને ઉકેલવામાં, રાત થોડી, વેશ ઝાઝા.
ને પછી એ ખેલવામાં, રાત થોડી, વેશ ઝાઝા.

થૈ ગયો છે ખેલ ચાલુ, દશ્ય તારું આવશે પણ;
જાતને શણગારવામાં, રાત થોડી, વેશ ઝાઝા.

દશ્ય સૌ ભજવાય છે, અંતિમ પળોમાં આંખ સામે,
કયાસ એનો કાઢવામાં, રાત થોડી, વેશ ઝાઝા.

મંચ પણ છે એ જ ને છે આયુધો પણ એ જ 'સુધીર',
છે ફરક સૌ નાચવામાં, રાત થોડી, વેશ ઝાઝા.

– સુધીર પટેલ

તમે બસ સાબદા રે'જે

અચાનક આવશે કાગળ, તમે બસ સાબદા રે'જે,
ખૂટી જશે બધાં અંજળ, તમે બસ સાબદા રે'જે.

નહીં જળ કે પછી મૃગજળ, તમે બસ સાબદા રે'જે.
ન આગળ કે કશું પાછળ, તમે બસ સાબદા રે'જે.

નહીં ફાવે કશીયે કળ, તમે બસ સાબદા રે'જે.
ખરી પડશે બધી અટકળ, તમે બસ સાબદા રે'જે.

ઉઘાડી ભીતરે સાંકળ, તમે બસ સાબદા રે'જે.
સિલકમાં એક કે બે પળ, તમે બસ સાબદા રે'જે.

વધી જશે રાગે ઝળહળ, તમે બસ સાબદા રે'જે.
ઉકેલીને સ્વયંના સળ, તમે બસ સાબદા રે'જે.

ગઝલ 'સુધીર' વહે ખળખળ, તમે બસ સાબદા રે'જે.
શબ્દનાં ફોડીને શ્રીફળ, તમે બસ સાબદા રે'જે.

- સુધીર પટેલ

Surendra Bhimani

108 Cherry Street, Jersey City, NJ 07305; he writes both poetry & prose in Gujarati, writes peoms in Chhand & Achhandas; he has translated poetry from Bangla & English into Gujarati and his translations have appeared in reputed magazines & newspapers in USA & India; his English writings have appeared in Georgia University Newspaper & in several publications in tri-state area; also he writes general & film-related articles and film reviews; his vast writings in various fields are waiting to be published; he writes TV-Scripts too. He wrote TV- Script based on old popular film songs for the Bombay Broadcasting TV Network program of the Tri-State Area around 1990s; he lives in USA for the last 25 years; he is a Journalist having M.A. in Journalism from University of Georgia and has experience in publishing & editorial; currently he works in The New Jersey State Judiciary.

સામીપ્ય

(વસંતતિલકા)

ઉત્કટ અતીવ મનમાં કંઈ ભાવ જગે,
જોઉં સમીપ પ્રિયને જ્યહીં મારી પાસે.
વીત્યા ઘણાં દિવસ કેવળ શૂન્યતામાં,
વેરાન ભૂમિ મનની જ પડી'તી સૂની.

બાળે બપોર રણના પટ શુષ્ક જેમ,
ધીખી રહ્યું'તું મન એમ જ હાય, મારું.
એમાં થઇ વીરડી એ મમ ઇષ્ટ આવ્યા,
છાઇ બધે શીતળતા પટ શુષ્કમાં એ.

હાયે, પરંતુ મધુ સખ્ય સધાય ના કૈં,
સામીપ્ય એ થઇ રહ્યું મન બાળનારું,
છે આટલા નજીક, અંતર તોય કેવું !
સંતાપ તેથી ઉરમાંહી થઇ રહ્યો છે.

ના દૈશ રે કદીય અંતર દુઃખ દાતા:
સામીપ્ય હોય, પરંતુ ન સખ્ય સાથે.

– સુરેન્દ્ર ભીમાણી

Viraf Kapadia

40, Parker Rd, Plainsboro, NJ 08536; he writes poems mostly in Gujarati, but in English too; he is fond of deep study of Indian & American literature; his poems appeared in American & Indian magazines; he believes, the art is for life, rather than art for the art's sake; he has one collection of his poems published.

ફૂવાના બે છેડા

ખુલ્લી આંખે
સાદી સમાધિ માંડીને
ઊભો છે ફૂવો.
ફૂવો તો ક્યાંય પણ જતો નથી,
ફૂવો તો કશુંય પ્રયોજતો નથી,
ફૂવો તો ઊભો છે એના ધ્યાન પર,
ફૂવો તો સીધો છે એના સ્થાન પર.

ફૂવાનો આકાશમુખી છેડો
જગત પર ઝૂકીને અલબેલો
પનિહારીઓનાં ગીત
ને વહુવારુઓની હળુ હળુ સૌ વાત
ધરે છે એના કાન પર;
કૃષકનું એકાંત ચરસ સંગીત
સંગ્રહે છે બખોલી પહાણ પર;

જલને આપે છે પ્રમાણમાં, હર્ષમાં હીલે છે;
સંગમરમર સિતારાઓની જમાતો,
રાતોની રાતો,
સીના પર ઝીલે છે;
પવન ને પંખી ને પર્ણ ને પતંગિયા સહ રમીને
તડકાના તેજબી અમીને ઝડપીને
ઉપર ને ઉપર ને ઉપર એ લસે છે.

જ્યારે અંદર ને અંદર જઇ વસે છે,
ઊંડો ને ઊંડો જે ધસે છે,
નીચે ને નીચે બસ ખસે છે....
ફૂવાનો પાતાળમુખી છેડો
ધરીને ચરણ નિજ સરવાણમાં
ઊતરતા ઊંડા ઉતરાણમાં
ધરતીના હ્રદયને પામવા
સ્થાન ને સમય સીમોલ્લંઘતો
અંધકારની ઉજિયારી ફંફોસતો
પોતાની સફરમાં ખૂંપેલો
ફૂવાનો પાતાળમુખી છેડો...
પોતે જે કહે છે, પોતે સુણે છે,
સ્વયં સ્વયં સહ ગણગણે છે,
પોતાની અંદર પોતાને બોલીને
પોતાને ખોઇને ખોળે છે પોતાને.

                                             — વિરાફ કાપડિયા

દાર્શનિક યાચક

મુખડા પર દીવાનો મોભો,
દેહડી પર પુરાણો ઝભ્ભો,
કરતલ પર પતરાનો ડબ્બો;
બોલ્યો બજારમાં ઊભેલો દાર્શનિક યાચક:
સાહેબ, સત્ય એવું હોય છે
જેવી મને માથા પર પડી છે ટાલ !
કહો, પડે જ છે ક્યારે કોઇનેય માથા પર ટાલ?
એ તો હોય જ છે ત્યાં હમેશાં,
હરિના
હર જનને માથે,
હર જનની સાથે,
હર જનને માટે,
ઢાંકીને માત્ર ઉગતા હોય છે
માયાવી જગતમાં વાળ !

- વિરાફ કાપડિયા

INDO-AMERICAN LITERARY ACADEMY'S

ANTHOLOGY OF POEMS (2005)

मराठी विभाग

कोडं

पहाटेच्या धूसर अंधारात भुरभुरणाऱ्या बर्फावर
पावलांची रांगोळी उमटवत जाताना
आठवतो पारिजाताचा भरगच्च सडा,
लक्ष वेचत असलेली मी आणि मन सुगंधून जाते

दुपारच्या लखख उन्हात जेंव्हा
बर्फाने लगडलेली झाडे चमचमतात
मला दिसतात श्रावणातली चिंब भिजलेली झाडे,
उंच उंच झोका आणि मन मोहरून जाते

सांयकाळच्या गुलाबी सावल्या
जेव्हा परावर्तित होतात सुस्तावणाऱ्या बर्फावरून
मी पाहत असते इंद्रधनुष्याचा झुला,
मावळत्या सुर्याला झुलवीत आणि मन रंगून जाते

रात्रीच्या शुभ्र चंद्रप्रकाशात मग
अभ्रकासारखा झगमगतो थंडावलेला हिमवर्षाव
मी जाते कोजागिरीच्या चांदण्यांत जागत राहते,
फेर धरून म्हणलेली गाणी आठवत आणि मन आनंदून जाते

हे अल्याडचे नाते पल्याडशी कसे जुळते
हे कोडं कधी उलगडेल कां ?

— अनुराधा आमलेकर

कालचक्र

पहाटेच्या घुक्यात आळसावलेलं आकाश
तडफडून पळत सुटतं, सुर्यकिरणाच्या प्रहाराने घुके झुगारत
सूर्य संतापाने फुलत असतो आणि पाहता पाहता:
प्रखर घगघगत्या उन्हात पडतो अस्ताव्यस्त डेरा

कितीहि गच्च मिटले डोळे तरी भगभगणारा प्रकाश कमी होत नाहीं
एक सुन्न बधिरता वळवळत जाते नसानसातून मेंदूकडे
आणि उद्या उजाडतो

'गुड मॉर्निंग' 'हाउ आर यू ?' ''फाइन' 'थँक यू.'
कढपुतळ्या सगळ्या मुखवटे चढवून
नाटक करायला सज्ज असतात

कॉम्प्युटर, फोन, कॉफी, फाईल्स उत्साहाने तरंगतात अवतीभवती
सूर्य मात्र हसत असतो खदखदा
आसूरी आनंदाने या साम्राज्यात गुलामावर कोरडे ओढत

अमानुष मने आसमंतात भरलेल्या
लाखो भुकेत्या जीवांचे टाहो दुर्लक्षित
भरल्या पोटी पैसे मोजत असतात
नवी कार नवी घरे घेण्याकरता
हा नाटकाचाच एक भाग आहे का ?

हा खेळ खेळून सूर्य ही कंटाळतो

त्याला दुसऱ्या साम्राज्याचा वेध-लागतो

इथली प्यादी कोलमडून पडली असतात

तो आपले आसूड उगारत दिशा फिरवतो

मांजराच्या पावलाने सायंकाळ येते जीवनांची

सोबत यमसावल्यांना घेऊन

त्यापाठोपाठ रात्रीची राणी येते काळोखाची शाल घेऊन

काही गुलामांनी दम-तोडला असतो, काही प्यादे मुखवट्यासहित गोठले

असतांत उरलेले शोधू पाहतात स्वत:चे अस्तित्व रात्रीच्या काळोखात

झापड भिरकाऊन टक्क डोळे उघडून

सगळ्यांना नसते मुभा ह्या राज्यात, डोळे मिटून स्वप्ने पाहण्याची

आणि काहि नशीबवान डोळे मिटतात कधी न उघडण्यासाठी

सूर्य खदखदा हसत असतो

दूसऱ्या साम्राज्यात तेजाने तळपत

आजचा उद्या करण्याकरिता

- अनुराधा आमलेकर

Dilip V. Chitre

6317 Merna Lane, Lanham, Md 20706-2862. He writes Marathi poems since many years and possesses interest in literature, social works, cultural and social activities, traveling, photography. His one collection of Marathi poems and two Act Musical play on Immigrant experiences have been published. He compiled a collection of Marathi short stories by NRI-writers and edited and re-written a book on The experiences of Iraq-Iran war by Dr. Gangadahr Maddiwar. By profession he is Architect [M.S.Univ. of Baroda] and presently working with U.S. Govt. Wash. D.C. as an Architect. He lives in USA for the last 34 yrs.

ब्रेन्ड कॅनिअन

एक नि:शब्द पोकळी
चहू बाजूंनी कानावर आदळणारा भयगंभीर सन्नाटा
ओंकारालाही आतल्याआंत घुसमटवणारा.

विखुरलेल्या गबतासारख्या दृष्टिसपाट शिखरांची
खोल खोल गाडलेली मुळे
सहस्रावधी वर्षांना मुकाट गिळून
अेखाद्या व्रतस्थ योग्यासारखी आभाळाला आव्हान देणारी.
ऊन-सावल्यांची अखंड बदलती मलमली लिंपण लेवून
रंगाचे थवे मांहेराला आल्यासारखे-विश्रब्ध.

मावळतीच्या बिंबाची अनेकविध रूपं
टोकाटोकांवर, कड्याकड्यांवर,

थेट तळापर्यंत घट्ट बिलगलेली
आणि त्या अव्याहत अभिसाराने लज्जांकित होऊन
अधिकच दूर गेलेले ताम्रवर्णी आकाश.
महारौद्र रूपी खळाळाचा थंडावून निपचित पडलेला
लांबच लांब कृश देह
भूतकाळाचा विसर पडलेला-
त्यानेच कोरलेल्या लेण्यांच्या तळाशी
समाधिस्थ असल्यासारखा.

समुद्राच्या लाटेला ओंजळित बंदिस्त करण्याच्या
केविलवाण्या धडपडीसारख्या
हे दृश्य उरांत साठवण्याच्या प्रयत्नांत-
खुजेपणाची जाणीव अधिकच तीव्र होऊन
भोवतालाच्या गर्दीत असून विलग असा
मी उभा.
विनम्र.
मुका.

-दिलीप वी. चित्रे

तरंगत तरंगत कोसळताना

तरंगत तरंगत कोसळताना
शांततेचा रंग लेवून
निस्तेज फिके आभाळ
सगळ्या आसमंतावर निपचित पसरलेले.
लपटलेले.

लयबद्ध भुरभुरीचा नि:शब्द भयाण सन्नाटा
संतत....
अविचल.... अखंड.... अष्टौप्रहर-
वाढत वाढत प्रलयकारी भितीने वेढून
क्षितिजापासून क्षितिजापर्यंत जडावत जाणाऱ्या
श्वेत-धवल आंच्छादना खाली
चिडीचिप.

पालवीहीन शुष्क भेदरलेले वृक्ष
आभाळभार तोलता तोलता
कोलमडणाऱ्या विजेचा खांबांना
आधार देत जीर्ण उभे-
फक्त आपल्या अस्तित्वाची साक्ष पटविण्याइतके
निरर्थक.

कुडकुडणारी झाडे-झुडुपे, गवत रस्ते
गाड्या घरे छपरे....
छपरांवरच्या धूर ओकणाऱ्या फायरप्लेसच्या चिमण्या-

झाडांवरली चिमण्यांची घरटी-खारींचे शेपटी उचांवत
टुकटुक डोळ्यांनी हिंस्त्र-गोंडस बघणे....
सफरचंदाच्या किडकिडीत फांद्यांना अवेळी फुटणारे
गोवर....
माणसा माणसांच्या मनांत उमटणारे
जगण्याचे अनाहूत हुंकार-
सगळे सगळे
आच्छादित आवरणाखाली मजबूत.
भयग्रस्त.
दारा-खिडक्यांचा किलकिल्या पडद्यांआडून
वेध घेत घेत
आकाशाच्या आवेगाचा अंदाज बांधणाऱ्या
भयभीत-करूणार्द्र-असहाय्य-अचेतन
नजरा
तेवढीच काय ती जिवंतपणाची खूण-
गोठलेली.

बाकी फक्त
तरंगत तरंगत कोसळताना
शांततेचा रंग लेवून
निस्तेज फिके आभाळ
सगळ्या आसमंतावर निपचित पसरलेले.
लपेटलेले.

-दिलीप वी. चित्रे

Dr. Kunda Joshi

8664, Belfry Drive, Philadelphia, PA 19128-1920. She loved poetry in her childhood and wrote several poems. Thereafter she is writing poems for the last 15 years Her poems have been presented in various literary programs. Her two collections of poems have been published. Her poems include gazals & songs too. Her songs are available with music in cassettes and CDs. For her literary contribution, she received The Award of Excellence from Brihan Maharashtra Mandal of North America. She is a Pediatrician by profession. She enjoys serving the poors and works in the Dept. of Public Health in Philadelphia.

कवी आणि व्यवहारज्ञानी

व्यवहारचतुर शहाण्याने कवीला बजावले,
पुन्हा पुन्हा फोड करुन समजावून सांगितले,

'चंद्राच्या चांदण्यावर नक्कोर पोट भरत नाही
विरही चक्रवाक रात्रभर रडत नाही
लुकलुकत्या तारकांनी अंधार दूर सरत नाही
स्वर्गीच्या अमृताने अमरत्व मिळत नाही
इंद्रधनूच्या रंगांनी दिवाणखाना सजत नाही
कस्तुरीच्या मृगाचा गंध कधी गवसत नाही !'

बिचारा वेडा कवी जरासा खिन्न झाला
मंदमधुर स्मित करीत क्षणातच उत्तरला,

'स्वप्नांच्या ओझ्यांनी पाठ माझी दमत नाही.
तारे मोजता अंधारांत काटा पायी खुपत नाही
कल्पनेच्या तीरावरील भरती कधी हटत नाही
अनुभूतीच्या स्पर्शाची पालवी कधी सुकत नाही...

हिरे माणिक मोती तुला लखलाभ होऊ देत
कल्पनांच्या रत्नराशी माझ्या मला राहू देत !'

- कुंदा जोशी

दोन पुण्यशील हात

दोन पुण्यशील हात
मुळीच कुरकुर न करता, शांतपणे अखंडित
राबतच राहणारे
चिमुकल्या संसाराचा योगक्षेम वाहणारे
दोन पुण्यशील हात

हातावरच्या असंख्य रेषा
भविष्याचे आलेख नव्हेत
जन्मभराच्या कष्टांची अबोल गाथा सांगणारे
दोन पुण्यशील हात

नव्हेत कुणा योद्ध्याचे
नव्हेत कुणा योग्याचे
नव्हेत कुणा मांत्रिकाचे
नव्हेत दैवी शक्तीचे

विनयाने जोडले, तरी मुळीच लाचार नसणारे
साधेसुधे संसारी, दोन पुण्यशील हात

वात्सल्याच्या उमाळ्याने पाठीवरून फिरणारे
काळ्याकुट्ट अंधारांत इवला दीप लावणारे
रुक्ष खडतर मातीमध्ये फुलबाग फुलवणारे
दोन पुण्यशील हात
दु:खाचे विष पचवून सुखच वाटीत राहणारे
दोन पुण्यशील हात

गोवर्धन स्थिरावला कृष्णाच्या अंगुलीवर?
तोलले म्हणे सारे जग शेषाच्या मस्तकावर
कपोलकल्पित कथा साऱ्या !
विश्वाचा सर्व भार जन्मभर सोसणारे
अनामिक, नगण्य
लाखो पुण्यशील हात
लाखो पुण्यशील हात

- कुंदा जोशी

Dr. Nilesh Savargaonkar

616 S. Dobbs Dell Street, Terre Haute, IN 47803; he writes Marathi poems, essays and articles since many years; he wrote essays/articles for the annual issues of Brihan Maharashtra Vritta for last 5 yrs. and edited as well as wrote essays for "Snehafulora" magazine for the last 5 yrs. He takes keen interest in promoting Marathi language and wrote extensive article on "Marathi" on internet [currently on "Marathi Maayboli" website]; he possesses Ph.D. in chemical Eng.

मैत्रपुष्प

जेव्हा आरशात प्रतिबिंब दिसले
चेहऱ्याची प्रथम ओळख पटली
इतर चेहरे ही तेव्हा वाचता आले
मग फुलली नवीन मैत्रीची फुले (१)

एकेक सुमने ती वेचून गोळा केली
पुष्पगुच्छाचे सौंदर्य वाढवत गेली
वाटलं, टिकतील ही अनंत काळी
राहू, एकत्रच, काष्ठी, पाषाणी, जळी (२)

पण अखेर ती चोहीकडे उधळली
निर्माल्य होऊन काळनदीत बुडाली
सुगंध हरपला, सुमने कोमेजली
गळून गेली एकेक मृदू पाकळी (३)

सदाफुली ताजी मात्र हाती राहिली
हृदयाच्या शिंपल्यात जपून ठेविली
काळाच्या पाण्यावर मनी जोपासली
मोती होऊन कोंदणात चमकली (४)

– निलेश सावरगावकर

दोन यज्ञ

एक यज्ञ मांडला द्रुपदाने
पेटवला सूडाच्या अग्निने
भूक त्याला द्रोणवधाची
आस होती धृष्टद्युम्नाची ॥ १ ॥

दुसरा यज्ञ नवयुगाचा
नेते व अतिरेकी राक्षसांचा
प्रजापतीना हाव संपत्तीची
राक्षसांना नशा धर्माची ॥ २ ॥

अतिरेकी रक्ताच्या थेंबातून
नवे रक्तबीज निर्माण होती
रक्तपिपासू नेत्यांकडून
वीर आगीत लोटले जाती ॥ ३ ॥

द्रुपदाच्या यज्ञाला होती
दूध-तूप-लोण्याची आहुती
नवयज्ञात निष्पाप जीव
शूरपुरुष बळी जाती ॥ ४ ॥

द्रुपदासम तुंबडी भरोनी
राहून रणापासून दूर
मांस इतरांचे खाऊनी
नवदानवांचे ढेकर क्रूर ॥ ५ ॥

द्रोणाचा वध करुन कपटाने
धृष्टद्युम्नादि षंढच ठरले
कोवळे जीव गिळुन बेपर्वाईने
नरराक्षस ते नपुंसक राहिले ।। ६ ।।

द्रुपदयज्ञातून वर आली
अनाहूत सुंदर पांचाली
लावण्याने कुरुकुळावरती
विनाशाक घाव करुन गेली ।। ७ ।।

नवयज्ञातून जी जन्मली
अपेक्षित बेफाम अशांतता
गिळंकृत करुन बसली
विश्वातील सारी मानवता ।। ८ ।।

– निलेश सावरगावकर

Prachi Divekar

2260 Par Lane, Apt. 1110, Willoughby, OH 44094-2951.

या वळणावर....

धुरकटलेल्या   वळणावरती
पुन्हा - पुन्हा मी वळून पाहते,
डोळ्यांमधले स्वप्नं एकटे
झरुन-सरुन ही उरुन राहते...

नव्या दमाचा श्वास घेऊनी
दूर दूर ही वाट चालते,
उलगडलेल्या ओंजळीत या
नक्षत्रांचे   दान घालते !

अनोळखी ही नक्षत्रे अन
वाटही पायतळीची नाही,
भरकटलेल्या   वळणावरचे
उगाच आठवत बसते काही...

अशाच भिजत्या वाटेवरती
असेच फिरुनी वळण मिळावे,
ओळख नक्षत्रांची पटावी,
अन वळणाशी सूर जुळावे....!

- प्राची दिवेकर

उडून गेलेली पाने...

झाड एकटेच उभे, त्याला नाही एक पान
मन आगीच्या धगीत, भोवताली मूक रान.....

कुठूनसा तिथं येई, पोपटांचा एक थवा,
झाड शोषूनही घेई, गर्द-हिरवी ती हवा...

झाड उदास एकटे, गर्भश्रीमंत जाहले,
दोन क्षणांचे सोबती, रावे तिथं विसावले !

मग घेऊन उडाले, जणू झाडाचीच पाने,
पानांविना झाड गाते, आता विरहाचे गाणे...!

- प्राची दिवेकर

Priti Pisolkar

10183 Parkwood Drive, Apt. 5, Cupertino, CA 95014.

कधी पासून?

तुझ्या-माझ्या 'आपल्या' चं
हे 'माझं-तुझं' कधीपासून ?
शरीरात वाहत्या रक्ताचं
हे असं गोठणं कधीपासून ?

तुझी माझी एकरुपता
शब्दांत न मावणारी...
मग भावनांना असं तराजूत
हे तोलणं रे कधीपासून ?

स्वप्नांमधे मुक्तपणे
आपल्या पाखरांचं फिरणं -
अन् अचानक व्यवहारी
हे असं बोलणं कधीपासून ?

तुझं-माझं दोघांचं,
अद्वैताचं नातं ना ?
मग हात सोडून अनोळखी,
हे चालणं रे कधीपासून ?

— प्रीती पिसोळकर

निसर्गाचं एक बरं आहे

निसर्गाचं एक बरं आहे
ढग दाटून आले की,
धारा होऊन बरसतात !
मनात दाटलेले कढ मात्र -
आतल्या - आत धुमसतात !!

मोकळ्या-मोकळ्या आकाशात
भिरभिरतात पाखरं -
चांदण्यांच्या सहवासात
डोलु लागते रात्रं !

डोंगरावरुन खाली -
झरझरतात झरे,
तुझ्यावाचून मी मात्र
कण - कण झुरे !

सागराच्या किनारी
झेपावतात लाटा -
दूर जंगलात जाणाऱ्या
वळणा - वळणाच्या वाटा !

पाना-पानाच्या साथीला...
फिरत्या वाऱ्याचे गाणे
शब्द ओठांवर येतानाही -
माझे हे गप्प रहाणे !

म्हणूनच वाटतं निसर्गाचं,
खरंच आपलं बर आहे -
तो मुक्तछंदी आणि....
माझं बंद दार आहे !

माझं बंद दार आहे......

- प्रीती पिसोळकर

Sandeep Chitre

21 Regal Drive, Monmouth Junction, NJ 08852; he writes Marathi poems; he loves playing flute and performing in dramas; he has master's in Computer Management and works as project Manager in Information Techonology; he lives in USA for the last 6 yrs.

मुक्त मोकळी

आज सामोरी सकाळ आली
मुक्त मोकळी छान हंसरी
झटकत जणू कुंतल ओले
नुकतीच नाहलेली ऋतुमती....

थोडा बोचरा शीतल असा
मंद सुगंधी पहाटवारा
निळ्या मोकळ्या पटलावरती
उघळीत होता रंगछटा....

साखरझोप पांधरत होती
स्वप्ने... ऊबदार घरट्यांमधूनी
कोण असा मी म्हणून भेटली?
मुक्त मोकळी सकाळ हंसरी
मुक्त मोकळी सकाळ हंसरी.....

— संदीप चित्रे

अमेरिका

आलो ह्या देशी जेंव्हा
ठाऊक नव्हते जराही तेंव्हा
आपणही असेच वागू, बोलू
आधी आलेल्यांसारखेचे करु १

येताना तर आपण म्हणालो
'आपण काय़ फार राहणार नाय'
चार बॅगा घेऊन आलो
जाऊ परत तसेच, त्यात काय?.... २

एक एक वर्ष सरत चालले
भारतभेटीचे स्वप्नंच राहिले
अमेरिकाच्या   शांततेत
इंडियाचे आवाज विरत चालले..... ३

सेकंड हँड गाडी झाली
आता नवीन गाडी हवी यार,
टोयोटा-होंडाच आपल्याला बेस्ट
अमेरिकन गाडच्यांचे नखरे फार ४

बदलले कपडे, बदलले वागणे
ऐक्सलंट सिंपल असते बोलणे
जिवलगांकडे   जातानाही
नकळत आधी फोन करणे.... ५

भारतात एच वनला वजन होते
इथे ग्रीन कार्डचे महत्व पटले
नकळत आपल्या गप्पांमधे
ग्रीन कार्डचे टप्पे आले..... ६

अजून किती वर्षे रेंट भरायचे ?
घराचा विचार तर करू
आमचे 'अपार्टमेंट कॉंप्लेक्स' म्हणणे थांबले
आमची 'डेव्हलपमेंट' म्हणू लागलो.....७

भारतात सगळयांना असेच वाटते
'तुमची तर ऐश आहे लेको'
तुम्हाला कसले त्रास-काळज्या?
खाओ, पीओ, मजे करो.....८

इथली धावपळ इथलेच जाणे इथले
ट्रॅफिक ही नकोसे होते कधी विचार
करता वाटते आपणच का ते जे
पुण्या-मुंबइतही मस्तीत जगलो ?....९

कसं सांगायचं इथे मिळणारा
प्रत्येक डॉलर बदल्यात काय करतो ?
डोक्यावर टांगती तलवार देतो
डोक्यावर टांगती तलवार देतो आणि
आईचा थरथरता हात मागतो....
आईचा थरथरता हात....मागतो
आईचा....थरथरता....हात मागतो....१०

– संदिप चित्रे

Sandhya Karnik

34645 Winslow Ter., Fremont, CA 94555; she graduted from Bombay University and received Gold Medal; she writes essays, short stories and poems; she published two books of collection of essays and short stories; her writings have been published in many Marathi magazines; she organized and conducted Woman's Support Group for 11 yrs. in Pennsylvania and for 4 yrs. in Florida; at present she is a volunteer for Hospice.

दोघी जणी

आईचा   निरोप   घेऊन
विशाल विमानाच्या पोटात बसून
ती   जेंव्हा   कोणत्याशा
अनोख्या प्रदेशात एकटीच निघाली
तेंव्हा आई येवढच म्हणाली...
जपून   बर   सदाफुली
धाडस   इतकच   कराव   की
त्याला पुरूनही आपण ऊराव...
नव   धाडस   करण्यासाठी...

ती जातच राहिली ठेचाळत...धडपडत...
झुंजत विजयी होत दमत...थकत...
कधी शिखरं सर करत नव्या वाटा शोधत
वादळ वाऱ्यात... अन स्वच्छ उन्हात
बहुधा एकटीच पण चालत राहिली

आज जरा स्वस्थपणे बसून मागे
वळून बघतां येत कसे निभावून
गेलो असही वाटून जातं
आज तिची चिमणी सोनकळी
निघाली आहे कुठल्याशा अज्ञात प्रदेशांत

युद्धाच्या भीषण छायेत होरपळणाऱ्या
मुलांची, भावंडांची काळजी घेण्यासाठी
बेचिराख घरासमोर थिजून बसलेल्या
आबाल वृद्धांसाठी... कुठेतरी अुघडच्या
आभाळाखाली ती निजेल, मैला
मैलाची वाट एकटीच चालेल...
घराबाहेर पडणाऱ्या तिच्या चिमणीला
ती येवढच म्हणाली जपून बर सदाफुली...
धाडस अितकच कराव की त्याला पुरूनही
आपण अुरावं नव धाडस करण्यासाठी....

- संध्या कर्णिक

वानप्रस्थ

तसं काहीच आपलं नसतं
वेगवेगळ्या   धर्मातल्या
निरनिराळ्या   संतांनी
हेच नाही का सांगितलं ?

जिथे   वाढलो,   खेळलो
ते   माहेरचं   घर
मागे वळून पाहिलं की
आपल नसतं राहिलेलं

जिथे   धावलो   बागडलो
तथा   कथित   ज्ञानाची
पदवी घेऊन बाहेर पडलो
ती शाळा देखिल आपली नसते

ज्या देशाच्या नागरिकत्वाचा
दाखला घेऊन बाहेर पडलो
तीस वर्षानंतर तो देशही
आपला राहिलेला नसतो

परत   जाऊन   पहावं   तर
रस्त्यांची नावं बदललेली
इमारती   उठवलेल्या
खाणा-खुणा पुसून गेलेल्या

हळू हळू लक्षात येतं
उन्हापावसात मायेने वाढवलेली
मुलं देखिल "So Long" म्हणत...
पंख पसरून उडालेली असतात

भोवतालच्या वस्तूंकडे पहावं
तर त्याही परक्या वाटतात
खिशात त्यांच्या पुराव्याच्या
रिसिटही असतात

तरी पण तसं काहीच नसतं आपलं
झाकोळून टाकणारं हे एकटेपण
सोबतीने येणारी विमनस्कता
ती तेवढी आपली असते

बिछान्यावर अंग टाकून
शेजारी, जाग्याच असलेल्या
जोडीदारकडे पहावं तर-
त्याचे डोळे तेच सांगतात

त्या निरव शांततेत
अन् वाढत्या अंधारात
आपण दोघे एकमेकांचे असतो
आपापला प्रवास करणारे
सहप्रवासी....

- संध्या कर्णिक

Shilpa Kelkar

11842 N. 91st Pl., Scottsdale, AZ 85255; she started writing Marathi poems recently; presently she focused her attention on writing poems of evolving relationship between mother and growing up daughter; she lives in USA for the last eight years and works as Retail Software Consultant.

तिच्या श्वासा- उच्छवासाला

तिच्या श्वासा-उच्छवासाला

असलेली निरागसतेची झालर

माझ्या मायेचा ओलावा

चिंब करून जाते…

तिच्या हाकेतून

प्रतित होणारी ओढ

माझ्या काळजाला हात घालते.

तिच्या श्वासातल्या निरागसतेत

आणि

तिच्या हाकेतल्या आर्ततेत

ताकद आहे माझ्यातल्या

कोवळीकेला फुलवण्याची….

मग मीही तिच्यासोबत

माझे विश्व लहान करून टाकते

तिच्या चिमुकल्या मिठीत सामावण्यासाठी !

- शील्पा केलकर

तशी मी मनाचीच....

तशी मी मनाचीच रचून गोष्ट सांगणाऱ्या पैकी एक...
सुरूवात करताना शेवट काय होईल याचा पत्ता नसलेली !
पूर्वी शेवट शोधता-शोधता मीच गोष्टीत हरवुन जात असे
पण आता मला तिच्या डोळ्यात 'पुढे काय' च्या खुणा दिसू लागतात...

तिच्या छोट्याशा कल्पनाविश्वाच्या भरारीचे पक्षी
उंच   उडत   असतात....आणि   अलगद्
मला गोष्टीच्या शेवटापाशी नेऊन सोडतात .....
आपोआपच उलगडत जाणारे तिचे आयुष्यच जणू काही....

अनोळखी प्रदेशातून सुरू झालेला तिचा-माझा प्रवास-
असाच   माझ्या   मनातल्या   गोष्टीसारखा......
'पुढे काय?' ची हुर हुर असतानाच नकळतपणे उलगडत जाणारा..

फक्त-

तिच्या डोळ्यातले 'संकेत' असेच मला वाचता येतील?
माझ्या मनातल्या या गोष्टीच्या तळाशी बुडून मी हे शोधत राहते....

- शील्पा केलकर

Shreenivas N. Mate

*2917 Tyler Ct. Simi Valley, CA 93063. He writes Marathi
poems and short stories and published in several magazines.
He has Bachelor's degree[Univ. of Mumbai] and Master's
degree[Kansas State Univ.] and works as Architect in Lose
Angeles since 1968. He lives in USA for the last 40 Yrs.*

स्वप्न

तें स्वप्न जीव घेणे
दुरूनी-मला-खुणावे
धरण्यास त्या पळावे
हाती न सापडे तें

दमुनी जरा बसावे
जवळून ते हंसावे
उठुनी पुन्हा पळावे
तें दूर दूर जाते

अन् शेवटी दयेने
ते थांबता जरासे
हातात ते धरावे
तें स्वप्न ना उरावे

- श्रीनिवास माटे

शब्दाविना-तुजला कळावे

या रिकाम्या कागदावर
अक्षरे जमवीत आहे
सुन्न कातर सांजवेळी
पत्र हे जुळवीत आहे.

ऐकती ना शब्द माझे
म्हणुन माझे मौन आहे
बोललो बोलूं नये ते
खोल हृदयी खंत आहे.

सांचले होते किती ते
वाहिले मी रिक्त आहे
त्यां पुराने बाग नेली
निपटलेला कांठ आहे.

शब्द हळवे हरपलेले
शोध त्यांचा फोल आहे
तेहि मज सोडून गेले
हे मनाला शल्य आहे.

पाठ-कोरी कागदाची
एक छोटी भेट आहे
शब्दाविना तुजला कळावा
तो मधोमध छाप आहे.

- श्रीनिवास माटे

Sujata Bhide
21230 Homestead Road, Apt. 5, Cupertino, CA 95014.

भेट

इतक्या वर्षांनी भेट झाली
मी मोकळेपणी हसलो,
तू मात्र नजरे मधली
वेदना लपवू शकली नाहीस

इतक्या वर्षांनी भेट झाली
मी भरभरून बोलत राहिलो,
तू मात्र हरवल्यासारखी
नुसतीच हसून पहात राहिलीस

होती कहाणी नेहेमीचीच तरी
आपण विसरणार नव्हतोच कधी,
तू मात्र आठवणींमधेच
गुंतून मिटून गेली होतीस

आता वाटतं - उगीच भेटलीस,
उगीच हुरहूर लावून गेलीस,
सुख शोधण्याचे माझे प्रयत्न
क्षणात धुळीला मिळवून गेलीस !

इतक्या वर्षांनी भेट झाली
आठवणींचे ढग दाटले,
तू मात्र इतका कसा

शांत, तृप्त, सुखी दिसलास ?
इतक्या वर्षांनी भेट झाली
तोंडून शब्दच फुटेना,
तू मात्र सारं विसरून
इतका कसा बोलत गेलास ?

होती कहाणी नेहेमीचीच खरी
विसरण्यातच शहाणपण होतं,
तू मात्र इतका कसा
सहज पुढे निधून गेलास ?

आता वाटतं - उगाच भेटलास,
उगाच इतका सुखी दिसलास,
साऱ्या स्मृती मी जपलेल्या
क्षणात मातीत मिसळून गेलास !

-सुजाता भिडे

होम-सिक

स्मृती म्हणजे स्वप्नासारखीच असते सुंदर जाणीव
एक सखोल, परिपूर्ण व्यापून टाकणारा अनुभव....
तिला केवळ शब्द-दृश्यांचा नसतो कधीच निर्बंध
तिला असतो.तिचा नाद, तिचा स्पर्श, नि गंध !

स्पर्श आईच्या हाताचा,
टोंचऱ्या दोरीच्या झोक्याचा,

उन्हात वाळणाऱ्या गव्हाचा,
बर्फ गोळ्याच्या चवीचा,
रिक्षाच्या जोरदार धक्क्याचा,
रेल्वेच्या कडक बाकाचा....

नाद देवळातल्या घंटेचा,
लग्नात घुमणाऱ्या सनईचा,
रात्री ओरडणाऱ्या कुत्र्यांचा,
पहाटे उठणाऱ्या पक्ष्यांचा,
कोंडीत अडकलेल्या गाड्यांचा,
मंडईत जमलेल्या गर्दीचा....

गंध जाई-मोगऱ्याचा,
पावसात भिजलेल्या मातीचा,
स्टेशनवरच्या वड्यांचा,
गाडीवरच्या चहाचा,
कचेरीतल्या पिवळट कागदांचा,
चौकातल्या धुरकट वाहनांचा.....

निसटत्या, पुसटशा, गच्च, खोल - कितीतरी आठवणी
चहूबाजूंनी भरून येतात अशा एखाद्या हळव्या क्षणी
दूर राहिली माणसं आणखी दूर राहिली आपली माती
इथे स्वप्नं परतीची आणि सोबत साऱ्या स्मृती
कधी रोखते भीती नकळत परतीचेही सारे यत्न
दिसले सारे तसेच की या स्मृती होऊनी राहातील स्वप्नं?

- सुजाता भिडे

Dr. Veena Shah
4124 Lakeridge Lane, Bloomfield Hills, MI 48302.

श्रावण

घननीळ दिवस जळधार
हातांवर मेंदी रंगे
थेंबथेंब झुलवीत
मी हरवून तुझिया संगे

पाऊसओले रान त्यावरी
सूर्य झळकती चिमणे
मन झाले हलूक निर्भर
ओठांवर हळवे गाणे

व्यापून पेटले प्राण
ही चढते हिरवी धून
की गंध धुंद-मातीचा
भोगावा डोळे मिटून.

– वीणा शाह

हेमंत

पैठण्यांच्या भराभर घड्या उलगडाव्या
तसे वृक्षांचे बदलते भरजरी रंग
केशरी, अंजिरी, गुलमोहरी
झळझळते मनोहारी अंग न् अंग

सोन्याच्या झिलईये राजस ऊन
सावल्यांचे मोहक लवलवते खेळ
झाडाझुडुपांना सावरेना फळभार
सफळ, संपूर्ण वाकलेले वेल

कधी उदास, कुंद, पाऊसझड
कधी निळे आभाळ, तरल मेघ
तृप्त भरलेल्या तळ्यांच्या आरशांत
बदकांची काळीकबरी रेखीव रेघ

डोळां दिपवणारा रंगाचा उत्सव
पानांच्या गालिचात अडखळले पाऊल
जीव रमून गेला झाडाफुलांत
तरी निष्पर्ण शिशिराची आलीच चाहूल.

– वीणा शाह

ॐॐॐॐ